DAILY RITUALS

SCHEME.

	Hours.	
MORNING. The *Question.* What good shall I do this day?	5 6 7	Rise, wash, and address *Powerful Goodness!* Contrive day's business, and take the resolution of the day; prosecute the present study, and breakfast.
	8 9 10 11	Work.
NOON.	12 1	Read, or look over my accounts, and dine.
AFTERNOON.	2 3 4 5	Work.
EVENING. The *Question.* What good have I done to-day?	6 7 8 9	Put things in their places. Supper. Music or diversion, or conversation. Examination of the day.
NIGHT.	10 11 12 1 2 3 4	Sleep.

Benjamin Franklin's ideal daily routine, from his autobiography

DAILY RITUALS

How Great Minds Make Time,
Find Inspiration, and Get to Work

Mason Currey

PICADOR

First published 2013 as a Borzoi Book by Alfred A. Knopf,
a division of Random House, Inc., New York,
and in Canada by Random House of Canada, Limited, Toronto

First published in Great Britain 2013 by Picador
an imprint of Pan Macmillan, a division of Macmillan Publishers Limited
Pan Macmillan, 20 New Wharf Road, London N1 9RR
Basingstoke and Oxford
Associated companies throughout the world
www.panmacmillan.com

ISBN 978-0-330-51249-7

3 5 7 9 8 6 4 2

A CIP catalogue record for this book is available from the British Library.

Printed and bound by CPI Group (UK) Ltd, Croydon, CR0 4YY

Visit www.picador.com to read more about all our books
and to buy them. You will also find features, author interviews and
news of any author events, and you can sign up for e-newsletters
so that you're always first to hear about our new releases.

FOR REBECCA

Who can unravel the essence, the stamp of the artistic temperament! Who can grasp the deep, instinctual fusion of discipline and dissipation on which it rests!

—THOMAS MANN, *Death in Venice*

CONTENTS

CONTENTS

CONTENTS

CONTENTS

INTRODUCTION

Nearly every weekday morning for a year and a half, I got up at 5:30, brushed my teeth, made a cup of coffee, and sat down to write about how some of the greatest minds of the past four hundred years approached this exact same task—that is, how they made the time each day to do their best work, how they organized their schedules in order to be creative and productive. By writing about the admittedly mundane details of my subjects' daily lives—when they slept and ate and worked and worried—I hoped to provide a novel angle on their personalities and careers, to sketch entertaining, small-bore portraits of the artist as a creature of habit. "Tell me what you eat, and I shall tell you what you are," the French gastronome Jean Anthelme Brillat-Savarin once wrote. I say, tell me what time you eat, and whether you take a nap afterward.

In that sense, this is a superficial book. It's about the circumstances of creative activity, not the product; it deals with manufacturing rather than meaning. But it's also, inevitably, personal. (John Cheever thought that you couldn't even type a business letter without revealing something of your inner self—isn't that the truth?) My underlying concerns in the book are issues that I struggle with in my own life: How do you do meaningful creative work while also earning a living? Is it better to devote yourself wholly to a project or to set aside a small portion of each day? And when there doesn't seem to be enough time for all you hope to accomplish, must you give things up (sleep, income, a clean house), or can you learn to condense activities, to do more in less time, to "work smarter, not harder," as my dad is always telling me? More broadly, are comfort and creativity incompatible, or is the opposite true: Is finding a basic level of daily comfort a prerequisite for sustained creative work?

I don't pretend to answer these questions in the following pages—probably some of them can't be answered, or can be resolved only individually, in shaky personal compromises—but I have tried to provide examples of how a variety of brilliant and successful people have confronted many of the same challenges. I wanted to show how grand creative visions translate to small daily increments; how one's working habits influence the work itself, and vice versa.

The book's title is *Daily Rituals,* but my focus in writing it was really people's *routines.* The word connotes ordinariness and even a lack of thought; to follow a routine is to be on autopilot. But one's daily routine is also a choice, or a whole series of choices. In the right hands, it can be a finely calibrated mechanism for taking advantage of a range of limited resources: time (the most limited resource of all) as well as willpower, self-discipline, optimism. A solid routine fosters a well-worn groove for one's mental energies and helps stave off the tyranny of moods. This was one of William James's favorite subjects. He thought you *wanted* to put part of your life on autopilot; by forming good habits, he said, we can "free our minds to advance to really interesting fields of action."

Ironically, James himself was a chronic procrastinator and could never stick to a regular schedule (see page 80).

As it happens, it was an inspired bout of procrastination that led to the creation of this book. One Sunday afternoon in July 2007, I was sitting alone in the dusty offices of the small architecture magazine that I worked for, trying to write a story due the next day. But instead of buckling down and getting it over with, I was reading *The New York Times* online, compulsively tidying my cubicle, making Nespresso shots in the kitchenette, and generally wasting the day. It was a familiar predicament. I'm a classic "morning person," capable of considerable focus in the early hours but pretty much useless after lunch. That afternoon, to make myself feel better about this often inconvenient predilection (who wants to get up at 5:30 *every day?*), I started searching the Internet for information about other writers' working schedules. These were easy to find, and highly entertaining. It occurred to me that someone should collect these anecdotes in one place—hence the *Daily Routines* blog I launched that very afternoon (my magazine story got written in a last-minute panic the next morning) and, now, this book.

The blog was a casual affair; I merely posted descriptions of people's routines as I ran across them in biographies, magazine profiles, newspaper obits, and the like. For the book, I've pulled together a vastly expanded and better researched collection, while also trying to maintain the brevity and diversity of voices that made the original appealing. As much as possible, I've let my subjects speak for themselves, in quotes from letters, diaries, and interviews. In other cases, I have cobbled together a summary of their routines from secondary sources. And when another writer has produced the perfect distillation of his subject's routine, I have quoted it at length rather than try to recast it myself. I should note here that this book would have been impossible without the research and writing of the hundreds of biographers, journalists, and scholars whose work I drew upon. I have documented all of my sources in the Notes section, which I hope will also serve as a guide to further reading.

Compiling these entries, I kept in mind a passage from a 1941 essay by V. S. Pritchett. Writing about Edward Gibbon, Pritchett takes note of the great English historian's remarkable industry—even during his military service, Gibbon managed to find the time to continue his scholarly work, toting along Horace on the march and reading up on pagan and Christian theology in his tent. "Sooner or later," Pritchett writes, "the great men turn out to be all alike. They never stop working. They never lose a minute. It is very depressing."

What aspiring writer or artist has not felt this exact sentiment from time to time? Looking at the achievements of past greats is alternately inspiring and utterly discouraging. But Pritchett is also, of course, wrong. For every cheerfully industrious Gibbon who worked nonstop and seemed free of the self-doubt and crises of confidence that dog us mere mortals, there is a William James or a Franz Kafka, great minds who wasted time, waited vainly for inspiration to strike, experienced torturous blocks and dry spells, were racked by doubt and insecurity. In reality, most of the people in this book are somewhere in the middle—committed to daily work but never entirely confident of their progress; always wary of the one off day that undoes the streak. All of them made the time to get their work done. But there is infinite variation in how they structured their lives to do so.

This book is about that variation. And I hope that readers will find it encouraging rather than depressing. Writing it, I often thought of a line from a letter Kafka sent to his beloved Felice Bauer in 1912. Frustrated by his cramped living situation and his deadening day job, he complained, "time is short, my strength is limited, the office is a horror, the apartment is noisy, and if a pleasant, straightforward life is not possible then one must try to wriggle through by subtle maneuvers." Poor Kafka! But then who among us can expect to live a pleasant, straightforward life? For most of us, much of the time, it is a slog, and Kafka's subtle maneuvers are not so much a last resort as an ideal. Here's to wriggling through.

DAILY RITUALS

W. H. Auden (1907-1973)

"Routine, in an intelligent man, is a sign of ambition," Auden wrote in 1958. If that's true, then Auden himself was one of the most ambitious men of his generation. The poet was obsessively punctual and lived by an exacting timetable throughout his life. "He checks his watch over and over again," a guest of Auden's once noted. "Eating, drinking, writing, shopping, crossword puzzles, even the mailman's arrival—all are timed to the minute and with accompanying routines." Auden believed that a life of such military precision was essential to his creativity, a way of taming the muse to his own schedule. "A modern stoic," he observed, "knows that the surest way to discipline passion is to discipline time: decide what you want or ought to do during the day, then always do it at exactly the same moment every day, and passion will give you no trouble."

Auden rose shortly after 6:00 A.M., made himself coffee, and settled down to work quickly, perhaps after taking a first pass at the crossword. His mind was sharpest from 7:00 until 11:30 A.M., and he rarely failed to take advantage of these hours. (He was dismissive of night owls: "Only the 'Hitlers of the world' work at night; no honest artist does.") Auden usually resumed his work after lunch and continued into the late afternoon. Cocktail hour began at 6:30 sharp, with the poet mixing himself and any guests several strong vodka martinis. Then dinner was served, with copious amounts of wine, followed by more wine and conversation. Auden went to bed early, never later than 11:00 and, as he grew older, closer to 9:30.

To maintain his energy and concentration, the poet relied on amphetamines, taking a dose of Benzedrine each morning the way many people take a daily multivitamin. At night, he used Seconal or another sedative to get to sleep. He continued this routine—"the chemical life," he called it—for twenty years, until the efficacy of the pills finally wore off. Auden regarded amphetamines as one of the "labor-saving devices" in the "mental kitchen," alongside alcohol, coffee, and tobacco—although he was well aware that "these mechanisms are very crude, liable to injure the cook, and constantly breaking down."

Francis Bacon (1909-1992)

To the outside observer, Bacon appeared to thrive on disorder. His studios were environments of extreme chaos, with paint smeared on the walls and a knee-high jumble of books, brushes, papers, broken furniture, and other detritus piled on the floor. (More agreeable interiors stifled his creativity, he said.) And when he wasn't painting, Bacon lived a life of hedonistic excess, eating multiple rich meals a day, drinking tremendous quantities of alcohol, taking whatever stimulants were handy, and generally staying out later and partying harder than any of his contemporaries.

Francis Bacon's London studio, 1971

And yet, as the biographer Michael Peppiatt has written, Bacon was "essentially a creature of habit," with a daily schedule that varied little over his career. Painting came first. Despite his late nights, Bacon always woke at the first light of day and worked for several hours, usually finishing around noon. Then another long afternoon and evening of carousing stretched before him, and Bacon did not dawdle. He would have a friend to the studio to share a bottle of wine, or he would head out for drinks at a pub, followed by a long lunch at a restaurant and then more drinks at a succession of private clubs. When evening arrived, there was a restaurant supper, a round of nightclubs, perhaps a visit to a casino, and often, in the early-morning hours, yet another meal at a bistro.

At the end of these long nights, Bacon frequently demanded that his reeling companions join him at home for one last drink—an effort, it seems, to postpone his nightly battles with insomnia. Bacon depended on pills to get to sleep, and he would read and reread classic cookbooks to relax himself before bed. He still slept only a few hours a night. Despite this, the painter's constitution was remarkably sturdy. His only exercise was pacing in front of a canvas, and his idea of dieting was to take large quantities of garlic pills and shun egg yolks, desserts, and coffee—while continuing to guzzle a half-dozen bottles of wine and eat two or more large restaurant meals a day. His metabolism could apparently handle the excessive consumption without dimming his wits or expanding his waistline. (At least, not until late in his life, when the drinking finally seemed to catch up with him.) Even the occasional hangover was, in Bacon's mind, a boon. "I often like working with a hangover," he said, "because my mind is crackling with energy and I can think very clearly."

Simone de Beauvoir (1908-1986)

"I'm always in a hurry to get going, though in general I dislike starting the day," Beauvoir told *The Paris Review* in 1965. "I first have tea and then, at about ten o'clock, I get under way and work until one. Then I see my friends and after that, at five o'clock, I go back to work and continue until nine. I have no difficulty in picking up the thread in the afternoon." Indeed, Beauvoir rarely had dif-

Simone de Beauvoir in her Paris apartment, 1976

ficulty working; if anything, the opposite was true—when she took her annual two- or three-month vacations, she found herself growing bored and uncomfortable after a few weeks away from her work.

Although Beauvoir's work came first, her daily schedule also revolved around her relationship with Jean-Paul Sartre, which lasted from 1929 until his death in 1980. (Theirs was an intellectual partnership with a somewhat creepy sexual component; according to a pact proposed by Sartre at the outset of their relationship, both partners could take other lovers, but they were required to tell each other everything.) Generally, Beauvoir worked by herself in the morning, then joined Sartre for lunch. In the afternoon they worked together in silence at Sartre's apartment. In the evening, they went to whatever political or social event was on Sartre's schedule, or else went to the movies or drank Scotch and listened to the radio at Beauvoir's apartment.

The filmmaker Claude Lanzmann, who was Beauvoir's lover from 1952 to 1959, experienced this arrangement firsthand. He described the beginning of their cohabitation in Beauvoir's Paris apartment:

> On the first morning, I thought to lie in bed, but she got up, dressed and went to her work table. "You work there," she said, pointing at the bed. So I got up and sat on the edge of the bed and smoked and pretended that I was working. I don't think she said a word to me until it was time for lunch. Then she went to Sartre and they lunched; sometimes I joined them. Then in the afternoon she went to his place and they worked three, maybe four hours. Then there were meetings, rendezvous. Later we met for dinner, and almost always she and Sartre would go to sit alone and she would offer the critique of what he wrote that day. Then she and I would come back to the [apartment] and go to sleep. There were no parties, no receptions, no bourgeois values. We completely avoided all that. There was the presence only of essentials. It was an uncluttered kind of life, a simplicity deliberately constructed so that she could do her work.

Thomas Wolfe (1900-1938)

Wolfe's prose has been criticized for its overindulgence and adolescent character, so it's interesting to note that the novelist practiced a writing ritual that was almost literally masturbatory. One evening in 1930, as he was struggling to recapture the feverish spirit that had fueled his first book, *Look Homeward, Angel,* Wolfe decided to give up on an uninspired hour of work and get undressed for bed. But, standing naked at his hotel-room window, Wolfe found that his weariness had suddenly evaporated and that he was eager to write again. Returning to the table, he wrote until dawn with, he recalled, "amazing speed, ease, and sureness." Looking back, Wolfe tried to figure out what had prompted the sudden change—and realized that, at the window, he had been unconsciously fondling his genitals, a habit from childhood that, while not exactly sexual (his "penis remained limp and unaroused," he noted in a letter to his editor), fostered such a "good male feeling" that it had stoked his creative energies. From then on, Wolfe regularly used this method to inspire his writing sessions, dreamily exploring his "male configurations" until "the sensuous elements in every domain of life became more immediate, real, and beautiful."

Wolfe typically began writing around midnight, "priming himself with awesome quantities of tea and coffee," as one biographer noted. Since he could never find a chair or table that was totally comfortable for a man of his height (Wolfe was 6'6"), he usually wrote standing up, using the top of the refrigerator as his desk. He would keep at it until dawn, taking breaks to smoke a cigarette at the window or pace through the apartment. Then he would have a drink and sleep until around 11:00. In the late morning Wolfe would begin another stretch of work, sometimes aided by a typist who would arrive to find the previous night's pages scattered all over the kitchen floor.

Patricia Highsmith (1921-1995)

The author of such psychological thrillers as *Strangers on a Train* and *The Talented Mr. Ripley* was, in person, as solitary and misanthropic as some of her heroes. Writing was less a source of pleasure for her than a compulsion, without which she was miserable. "There is no real life except in working, that is to say in the imagination," she wrote in her journal. Fortunately, Highsmith was rarely short of inspiration; she had ideas, she said, like rats have orgasms.

Highsmith wrote daily, usually for three or four hours in the morning, completing two thousand words on a good day. The biographer Andrew Wilson records her methods:

> Her favourite technique to ease herself into the right frame of mind for work was to sit on her bed surrounded by cigarettes, ashtray, matches, a mug of coffee, a doughnut and an accompanying saucer of sugar. She had to avoid any sense of discipline and make the act of writing as pleasurable as possible. Her position, she noted, would be almost foetal

Patricia Highsmith, Paris, 1977

and, indeed, her intention was to create, she said, "a womb of her own."

Highsmith was also in the habit of having a stiff drink before she started to write—"not to perk her up," Wilson notes, "but to reduce her energy levels, which veered toward the manic." In her later years, as she became a hardened drinker with a high tolerance, she kept a bottle of vodka by her bedside, reaching for it as soon as she woke and marking the bottle to set her limit for the day. She was also a chain smoker for most of her life, going through a pack of Gauloises a day. In matters of food, she was indifferent. One acquaintance remembered that "she only ever ate American bacon, fried eggs and cereal, all at odd times of the day."

Ill at ease around most people, she had an unusually intense connection with animals—particularly cats, but also snails, which she bred at home. Highsmith was inspired to keep the gastropods as pets when she saw a pair at a fish market locked in a strange embrace. (She later told a radio interviewer that "they give me a sort of tranquility.") She eventually housed three hundred snails in her garden in Suffolk, England, and once arrived at a London cocktail party carrying a gigantic handbag that contained a head of lettuce and a hundred snails—her companions for the evening, she said. When she later moved to France, Highsmith had to get around the prohibition against bringing live snails into the country. So she smuggled them in, making multiple trips across the border with six to ten of the creatures hidden under each breast.

Federico Fellini (1920–1993)

The Italian filmmaker claimed that he was unable to sleep for more than three hours at a time. In a 1977 interview, he described his morning routine:

> I'm up at six in the morning. I walk around the house, open windows, poke around boxes, move books from here to there. For years I've been trying to make myself a decent cup of coffee, but it's not one of my specialties. I go downstairs, outside as soon as possible. By seven I'm on the telephone. I'm scrupulous about choosing who it's safe to wake at seven in the morning without their getting insulted.

For some I perform a real service, a wake-up service;
they become used to my waking them at seven or so.

Fellini wrote for newspapers as a young man, but
he found that his temperament was better suited to the
movies—he liked the sociability of the filmmaking process. "A writer can do everything by himself—but he
needs discipline," he said. "He has to get up at seven in
the morning, and be alone in a room with a white sheet
of paper. I am too much of a *vitellone* [loafer] to do that.
I think I have chosen the best medium of expression for
myself. I love the very precious combination of work and
of living-together that filmmaking offers."

Ingmar Bergman (1918-2007)

"Do you know what moviemaking is?" Bergman asked
in a 1964 interview. "Eight hours of hard work each day
to get three minutes of film. And during those eight hours
there are maybe only ten or twelve minutes, if you're
lucky, of real creation. And maybe they don't come.
Then you have to gear yourself for another eight hours
and pray you're going to get your good ten minutes this
time." But moviemaking for Bergman was also writing
scripts, which he always did in his home on the remote
island of Fårö, Sweden. There he followed essentially the
same schedule for decades: up at 8:00, writing from 9:00
until noon, then an austere meal. "He constantly eats the
same lunch," the actress Bibi Andersson remembered. "It
doesn't change. It's some kind of whipped sour milk, very

fat, and strawberry jam, very sweet—a strange kind of baby food he eats with corn flakes."

After lunch, Bergman worked again from 1:00 to 3:00, then slept for an hour. In the late afternoon he went for a walk or took the ferry to a neighboring island to pick up the newspapers and the mail. In the evening he read, saw friends, screened a movie from his large collection, or watched TV (he was particularly fond of *Dallas*). "I never use drugs or alcohol," Bergman said. "The most I drink is a glass of wine and that makes me incredibly happy." Music was also "absolutely necessary" for him, and Bergman enjoyed everything from Bach to the Rolling Stones. As he got older, he had trouble sleeping, never managing more than four or five hours a night, which made shooting films arduous. But even after he retired from filmmaking in 1982, Bergman continued to make television movies, direct plays and operas, and write plays, novels, and a memoir. "I have been working all the time," he said, "and it's like a flood going through the landscape of your soul. It's good because it takes away a lot. It's cleansing. If I hadn't been at work all the time, I would have been a lunatic."

Morton Feldman (1926-1987)

A French journalist visited Feldman in 1971, when the American composer was taking a month to work in a small village about an hour north of Paris. "I live here like a monk," Feldman said.

I get up at six in the morning. I compose until eleven, then my day is over. I go out, I walk, tirelessly, for hours. Max Ernst is not far away. [John] Cage also came here. I'm cut off from all other activity. What effect does that have on me?

Very good . . . But I'm not used to having so much time, so much ease. Usually I create in the midst of a lot of bustle, of work. You know, I always worked at something other than music. My parents were in "business" and I participated in their worries, in their life. . . .

Then, I got married, my wife had a very good job and she was out all day. I got up at six in the morning, I did the shopping, the meals, the housework, I worked like mad and in the evening we received a lot of friends (I had so many friends without even realizing it myself). At the end of the year, I discovered that I had not written a single note of music!

When he did find the time to compose, Feldman employed a strategy that John Cage taught him—it was "the most important advice anybody ever gave me," Feldman told a lecture audience in 1984. "He said that it's a very good idea that after you write a little bit, stop and then copy it. Because while you're copying it, you're thinking about it, and it's giving you other ideas. And that's the way I work. And it's marvelous, just wonderful, the relationship between working and copying." External conditions—having the right pen, a good chair—were important, too. Feldman wrote in a 1965 essay, "My concern at times is nothing more than establishing a series of practical considerations that will enable me to work. For years I said if I could only find a comfortable chair I would rival Mozart."

Wolfgang Amadeus Mozart (1756-1791)

In 1781, after several years searching in vain for a suitable post with the European nobility, Mozart decided to settle in Vienna as a freelance composer and performer. There were ample opportunities in the city for a musician of Mozart's talent and renown, but staying solvent necessitated a frantic round of piano lessons, concert performances, and social visits with the city's wealthy patrons. At the same time, Mozart was also courting his future wife, Constanze, under the disapproving gaze of her mother. All this activity left him only a few hours a day to compose new works. In a 1782 letter to his sister, he gave a detailed account of these hectic days in Vienna:

> My hair is always done by six o'clock in the morning and by seven I am fully dressed. I then compose until nine. From nine to one I give lessons. Then I lunch, unless I am invited to some house where they lunch at two or even three o'clock, as, for example, today and tomorrow at Countess Zichy's and Countess Thun's. I can never work before five or six o'clock in the evening, and even then I am often prevented by a concert. If I am not prevented, I compose until nine. I then go to my dear Constanze, though the joy of seeing one another is nearly always spoilt

by her mother's bitter remarks. . . . At half past ten or eleven I come home—it depends on her mother's darts and on my capacity to endure them! As I cannot rely on being able to compose in the evening owing to the concerts which are taking place and also to the uncertainty as to whether I may not be summoned now here and now there, it is my custom (especially if I get home early) to compose a little before going to bed. I often go on writing until one—and am up again at six.

"Altogether I have so much to do that often I do not know whether I am on my head or my heels," Mozart wrote to his father. Apparently he was not exaggerating; when Leopold Mozart went to visit his son a few years later, he found the freelancer's life just as tumultuous as promised. He wrote home from Vienna, "It is impossible for me to describe the rush and bustle."

Ludwig van Beethoven (1770-1827)

Beethoven rose at dawn and wasted little time getting down to work. His breakfast was coffee, which he prepared himself with great care—he determined that there should be sixty beans per cup, and he often counted them out one by one for a precise dose. Then he sat at his desk and worked until 2:00 or 3:00, taking the occasional break to walk outdoors, which aided his creativity. (Perhaps for this reason, Beethoven's productivity was generally higher during the warmer months.)

After a midday dinner, Beethoven embarked on a long, vigorous walk, which would occupy much of the rest of the afternoon. He always carried a pencil and a couple of sheets of music paper in his pocket, to record chance musical thoughts. As the day wound down, he might stop at a tavern to read the newspapers. Evenings were often spent with company or at the theater, although in winter he preferred to stay home and read. Supper was usually a simple affair—a bowl of soup, say, and some leftovers from dinner. Beethoven enjoyed wine with his food, and he liked to have a glass of beer and a pipe after supper. He rarely worked on his music in the evening, and he retired early, going to bed at 10:00 at the latest.

Beethoven's unusual bathing habits are worth noting here. His pupil and secretary Anton Schindler recalled them in the biography *Beethoven As I Knew Him*:

Washing and bathing were among the most pressing necessities of Beethoven's life. In this respect he was indeed an Oriental: to his way of thinking Mohammed did not exaggerate a whit in the number of ablutions he prescribed. If he did not dress to go out during the morning working hours, he would stand in great *déshabillé* at his washstand and pour large pitchers of water over his hands, bellowing up and down the scale or sometimes humming loudly to himself. Then he would stride around his room with rolling or staring eyes, jot something down, then resume his pouring of water and loud singing. These were moments of deep meditation, to which no one could have objected but for two unfortunate consequences. First of all, the servants would often burst out laughing. This made the master angry and he would sometimes assault them in language that made him cut an even more ridiculous figure. Or, secondly, he would come into conflict with the landlord, for all too often so much water was spilled that it went right through the floor. This was one of the main reasons for Beethoven's unpopularity as a tenant. The floor of his living-room would have had to be covered with asphalt to prevent all that water from seeping through. And the master was totally unaware of the excess of inspiration under his feet!

Søren Kierkegaard (1813-1855)

The Danish philosopher's day was dominated by two pursuits: writing and walking. Typically, he wrote in the morning, set off on a long walk through Copenhagen at noon, and then returned to his writing for the rest of the day and into the evening. The walks were where he had his best ideas, and sometimes he would be in such a hurry to get them down that, returning home, he would write standing up before his desk, still wearing his hat and gripping his walking stick or umbrella.

Kierkegaard kept up his energy with coffee, usually taken after supper and a glass of sherry. Israel Levin, his secretary from 1844 until 1850, recalled that Kierkegaard owned "at least fifty sets of cups and saucers, but only one of each sort"—and that, before coffee could be served,

Levin had to select which cup and saucer he preferred that day, and then, bizarrely, justify his choice to Kierkegaard. And this was not the end of the strange ritual. The biographer Joakim Garff writes:

> Kierkegaard had his own quite peculiar way of having coffee: Delightedly he seized hold of the bag containing the sugar and poured sugar into the coffee cup until it was piled up above the rim. Next came the incredibly strong, black coffee, which slowly dissolved the white pyramid. The process was scarcely finished before the syrupy stimulant disappeared into the magister's stomach, where it mingled with the sherry to produce additional energy that percolated up into his seething and bubbling brain—which in any case had already been so productive all day that in the half-light Levin could still notice the tingling and throbbing in the overworked fingers when they grasped the slender handle of the cup.

Voltaire (1694-1778)

The French Enlightenment writer and philosopher liked to work in bed, particularly in his later years. A visitor recorded Voltaire's routine in 1774: He spent the morning in bed, reading and dictating new work to one of his secretaries. At noon he rose and got dressed. Then he would receive visitors or, if there were none, continue to work, taking coffee and chocolate for sustenance. (He did not eat lunch.) Between 2:00 and 4:00, Voltaire and his principal secretary, Jean-Louis Wagnière, went out in a carriage to survey the estate. Then he worked again until 8:00, when he would join his widowed niece (and longtime lover) Madame Denis and others for supper. But his working day did not end there. Voltaire often continued to give dictation after supper, continuing deep into the night. Wagnière estimated that, all told, they worked eighteen to twenty hours a day. For Voltaire, it was a perfect arrangement. "I love the cell," he wrote.

Benjamin Franklin (1706-1790)

In his *Autobiography,* Franklin famously outlined a scheme to achieve "moral perfection" according to a thirteen-week plan. Each week was devoted to a particular virtue—temperance, cleanliness, moderation, et cetera— and his offenses against these virtues were tracked on a calendar. Franklin thought that if he could maintain his devotion to one virtue for an entire week, it would become a habit; then he could move on to the next virtue, successively making fewer and fewer offenses (indicated on the calendar by a black mark) until he had completely reformed himself and would thereafter need only occasional bouts of moral maintenance.

The plan worked, up to a point. After following the course several times in a row, he found it necessary to go through just one course in a year, and then one every few years. But the virtue of *order*—"Let all your things have their places; let each part of your business have its time"—appears to have eluded his grasp. Franklin was not naturally inclined to keep his papers and other possessions organized, and he found the effort so vexing that he almost quit in frustration. Moreover, the demands of his printing business meant that he couldn't always follow the exacting daily timetable that he set for himself. That ideal schedule, also recorded in Franklin's little book of virtues, looked like this:

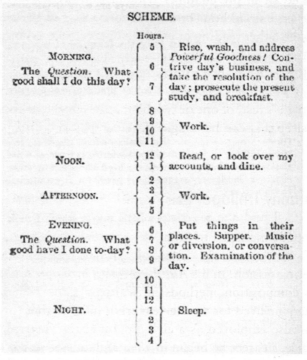

Benjamin Franklin's ideal daily routine, from his autobiography

This timetable was formulated before Franklin adopted a favorite habit of his later years—his daily "air bath." At the time, baths in cold water were considered a tonic, but Franklin believed the cold was too much of a shock to the system. He wrote in a letter:

I have found it much more agreeable to my constitution to bathe in another element, I mean cold air. With this view I rise early almost every morning, and sit in my chamber without any clothes whatever, half an hour or an hour, according to the season, either reading or writing. This practice is not in the least painful, but on the contrary, agreeable; and if I return to bed afterwards, before I dress myself, as sometimes happens, I make a supplement to my night's rest, of one or two hours of the most pleasing sleep that can be imagined.

Anthony Trollope (1815-1882)

Trollope managed to produce forty-seven novels and sixteen other books by dint of an unvarying early-morning writing session. In his *Autobiography,* Trollope described his composition methods at Waltham Cross, England, where he lived for twelve years. For most of that time he was also employed as a civil servant at the General Post Office, a career he began in 1834 and did not resign until thirty-three years later, when he had already published more than two dozen books.

It was my practice to be at my table every morning at 5.30 A.M.; and it was also my practice to allow myself no mercy. An old groom, whose business it was to call me, and to whom I paid £5 a year extra for the duty, allowed himself no mercy. During all those years at Waltham Cross he never was once late with the coffee which it was his duty to bring me. I do not know that I ought not to feel that I owe more to him than to any one else for the success I have had. By beginning at that hour I could complete my literary work before I dressed for breakfast.

All those I think who have lived as literary men,—working daily as literary labourers,—will agree with me that three hours a day will produce as much as a man ought to write. But then, he should so have trained himself that he shall be able to work continuously during those three hours,—so have tutored his mind that it shall not be necessary for him to sit nibbling his pen, and gazing at the wall before him, till he shall have found the words with which he wants to express his ideas. It had at this time become my custom,—and is still my custom, though of late I have become a little lenient of myself,—to write with my watch before me, and to require of myself 250 words every quarter of an hour. I have found that the 250 words have been forthcoming as regularly as my watch went. But my three hours were not devoted entirely to writing. I always began my task by reading the work of the day before, an operation which would take me half an hour, and which consisted chiefly in weighing with my ear the sound of the words and phrases. . . .

This division of time allowed me to produce over ten pages of an ordinary novel volume a day, and if kept up through ten months, would have given as its results three novels of three volumes each in the year;—the precise amount which so greatly acerbated the publisher in Paternoster Row, and which must at any rate be felt to be quite as much as the novel-readers of the world can want from the hands of one man.

If he completed a novel before his three hours were up, Trollope would take out a fresh sheet of paper and immediately begin the next one. In his industrious habits he was no doubt influenced by his mother, Frances Trollope, an immensely popular author in her own right. She did not begin writing until the age of fifty-three, and then only because she desperately needed money to support her six children and ailing husband. In order to squeeze the necessary writing time out of the day while still acting as the primary caregiver to her family, Mrs. Trollope sat down at her desk each day at 4:00 A.M. and completed her writing in time to serve breakfast.

Jane Austen (1775-1817)

Austen never lived alone and had little expectation of solitude in her daily life. Her final home, a cottage in the village of Chawton, England, was no exception: she lived there with her mother, her sister, a close friend, and three servants, and there was a steady stream of visitors, often unannounced. Nevertheless, between settling in Chawton in 1809 and her death, Austen was remarkably productive: she revised earlier versions of *Sense and Sensibility* and *Pride and Prejudice* for publication, and wrote three new novels, *Mansfield Park, Emma,* and *Persuasion.*

Austen wrote in the family sitting room, "subject to all kinds of casual interruptions," her nephew recalled.

> She was careful that her occupation should not be suspected by servants, or visitors, or any persons beyond her own family party. She wrote upon small sheets of paper which could easily be put away, or covered with a piece of blotting paper. There was, between the front door and the offices, a swing door which creaked when it was opened; but she objected to having this little inconvenience remedied, because it gave her notice when anyone was coming.

Austen rose early, before the other women were up, and played the piano. At 9:00 she organized the family breakfast, her one major piece of household work. Then she settled down to write in the sitting room, often with her mother and sister sewing quietly nearby. If visitors showed up, she would hide her papers and join in the sewing. Dinner, the main meal of the day, was served between 3:00 and 4:00. Afterward there was conversation, card games, and tea. The evening was spent reading aloud from novels, and during this time Austen would read her work-in-progress to her family.

Although she did not have the independence and privacy that a contemporary writer might expect, Austen was nonetheless fortunate with the arrangements at

Chawton. Her family was respectful of her work, and her sister Cassandra shouldered the bulk of the house-running burden—a huge relief for the novelist, who once wrote, "Composition seems to me impossible with a head full of joints of mutton & doses of rhubarb."

Frédéric Chopin (1810-1849)

During his ten-year relationship with the French novelist George Sand, Chopin spent most of his summers at Sand's country estate in Nohant, in central France. Chopin was an urban animal; in the country, he quickly became bored and moody. But the lack of distractions was good for his music. Most days he rose late, had breakfast in his bedroom, and spent the day composing, with a break to give a piano lesson to Sand's daughter, Solange. At 6:00 P.M. the household assembled for dinner, often served outdoors, followed by music, conversation, and sundry entertainments. Then Chopin retired to bed while Sand went to her writing table (see p. 156).

Although his lack of any real responsibility at Nohant made it easier for Chopin to compose, his work process was still far from effortless. Sand noted his work habits:

His creation was spontaneous and miraculous. He found it without seeking it, without foreseeing it. It came on his piano suddenly, complete, sublime, or it sang in his head during a walk, and he was impatient to play it to himself. But then began the most heart-rending labour I ever saw. It was a series

Frédéric Chopin sketched by George Sand,
circa 1842

of efforts, of irresolutions, and of frettings to seize
again certain details of the theme he had heard;
what he had conceived as a whole he analysed too
much when wishing to write it, and his regret at
not finding it again, in his opinion, clearly defined,
threw him into a kind of despair. He shut himself
up in his room for whole days, weeping, walking,
breaking his pens, repeating and altering a bar
a hundred times, writing and effacing it as many
times, and recommencing the next day with a minute and desperate perseverance. He spent six weeks
over a single page to write it at last as he had noted
it down at the very first.

Sand tried to convince Chopin to trust his initial inspiration, but he was loath to take her advice, and became angry when disturbed. "I dared not insist," Sand wrote. "Chopin when angry was alarming, and as, with me, he always restrained himself, he seemed almost to choke and die."

Gustave Flaubert (1821-1880)

Flaubert began writing *Madame Bovary* in September 1851, shortly after returning to his mother's house in Croisset, France. He had spent the previous two years abroad, traveling through the Mediterranean region, and the long journey seems to have satisfied his youthful yearning for adventure and passion. Now, just shy of his thirtieth birthday—and already looking middle-aged,

Gustave Flaubert's study at Croisset

with a large paunch and rapidly thinning hair—Flaubert felt capable of the discipline necessary for writing his new book, which would marry a humble subject matter to a rigorous and exacting prose style.

The book gave him trouble from the start. "Last night I began my novel," he wrote his longtime correspondent and lover, Louise Colet. "Now I foresee terrifying difficulties of style. It's no easy business to be simple." In order to concentrate on the task, Flaubert established a strict routine that allowed him to write for several hours each night—he was easily distracted by noises in the daytime—while also fulfilling some basic familial obligations. (At the Croisset house there were, in addition to the author and his doting mother, Flaubert's precocious five-year-old niece, Caroline; her English governess; and, frequently, Flaubert's uncle.)

Flaubert woke at 10:00 each morning and rang for the servant, who brought him the newspapers, his mail, a glass of cold water, and his filled pipe. The servant's bell also served as notice for the rest of the family that they could cease creeping about the house and speaking in low voices in order not to disturb the slumbering author. After Flaubert had opened his letters, drank his water, and taken a few puffs of his pipe, he would pound on the wall above his head, a signal for his mother to come in and sit on the bed beside him for an intimate chat until he decided to get up. Flaubert's morning toilet, which included a very hot bath and the application of a tonic that was supposed to arrest hair loss, would be completed by 11:00, at which time he would join the family in the dining room for a late-morning meal that served as both his breakfast and his lunch. The author didn't like to work on a full stomach, so he ate a relatively light repast, typically consisting of eggs, vegetables, cheese or fruit, and a cup of cold chocolate. Then the family moved outdoors for a stroll, often ascending a hill behind the house to a terrace that overlooked the Seine, where they would gossip, argue, and smoke under a stand of chestnut trees.

At 1:00, Flaubert commenced his daily lesson to Caroline, which took place in his study, a large room with bookcases crammed with books, a sofa, and a white bearskin rug. The governess was in charge of Caroline's English education, so Flaubert limited his lessons to history and geography, a role that he took very seriously. After an hour of instruction, Flaubert dismissed his pupil and settled into the high-backed armchair in front of his large round table and did some work—mostly reading, it seems—until dinner at 7:00. After a meal, he sat and talked with his mother until 9:00 or 10:00, when she went to bed. Then his real work began. Hunched over his table while the rest of the household slept, the "hermit of Croisset" struggled to forge a new prose style, one stripped of all unnecessary ornament and excessive emotion in favor of merciless realism rendered in precisely the right words. This word-by-word and sentence-by-sentence labor proved almost unbearably difficult:

> Sometimes I don't understand why my arms don't drop from my body with fatigue, why my brain doesn't melt away. I am leading an austere life, stripped of all external pleasure, and am sustained only by a kind of permanent frenzy, which sometimes makes me weep tears of impotence but never abates. I love my work with a love that is frantic and per-

verted, as an ascetic loves the hair shirt that scratches his belly. Sometimes, when I am empty, when words don't come, when I find I haven't written a single sentence after scribbling whole pages, I collapse on my couch and lie there dazed, bogged down in a swamp of despair, hating myself and blaming myself for this demented pride that makes me pant after a chimera. A quarter of an hour later, everything has changed; my heart is pounding with joy.

Often he complained of his slow progress. "*Bovary* is not exactly racing along: two pages in a week! Sometimes I'm so discouraged I could jump out a window." But, gradually, the pages began to pile up. On Sundays, his good friend Louis Bouilhet would visit and Flaubert would read aloud his week's progress. Together they would go over sentences dozens, even hundreds, of times until they were just right. Bouilhet's suggestions and encouragement bolstered Flaubert's confidence and helped calm his frazzled nerves for another week of slow, torturous composition. This monotonous daily struggle continued, with few breaks, until June 1856, when, after nearly five years of labor, Flaubert finally mailed the manuscript to his publisher. And yet, as difficult as the writing was, it was in many ways an ideal life for Flaubert. "After all," as he wrote years later, "work is still the best way of escaping from life!"

Henri de Toulouse-Lautrec (1864-1901)

Toulouse-Lautrec did his best creative work at night, sketching at cabarets or setting up his easel in brothels. The resulting depictions of fin de siècle Parisian nightlife made his name, but the cabaret lifestyle proved disastrous to his health: Toulouse-Lautrec drank constantly and slept little. After a long night of drawing and binge-drinking, he would often wake early to print lithographs, then head to a café for lunch and several glasses of wine. Returning

Henri de Toulouse-Lautrec in his studio in 1894, in front of his painting In the Salon of the Rue des Moulins. *Mireille (with the spear) is the painting's main subject, sitting in the foreground with her knee drawn up.*

to his studio, he would take a nap to sleep off the wine, then paint until the late afternoon, when it was time for aperitifs. If there were visitors, Toulouse-Lautrec would proudly mix up a few rounds of his infamous cocktails; the artist was smitten with American mixed drinks, which were still a novelty in France at the time, and he liked to invent his own concoctions—assembled not for complementary flavors but for their vivid colors and extreme potency. (One of his inventions was the Maiden Blush, a combination of absinthe, mandarin, bitters, red wine, and champagne. He wanted the sensation, he said, of "a peacock's tail in the mouth.") Dinner, more wine, and another night of boozy revelry soon followed. "I expect to burn myself out by the time I'm forty," Toulouse-Lautrec told an acquaintance. In reality, he only made it to thirty-six.

Thomas Mann (1875–1955)

Mann was always awake by 8:00 A.M. After getting out of bed, he drank a cup of coffee with his wife, took a bath, and dressed. Breakfast, again with his wife, was at 8:30. Then, at 9:00, Mann closed the door to his study, making himself unavailable for visitors, telephone calls, or family. The children were strictly forbidden to make any noise between 9:00 and noon, Mann's prime writing hours. It was then that his mind was freshest, and Mann placed tremendous pressure on himself to get things down during that time. "Every passage becomes a 'passage,'" he wrote, "every adjective a decision." Anything that didn't

Thomas Mann, New York City, 1943

come by noon would have to wait until the next day, so
he forced himself to "clench the teeth and take one slow
step at a time."

His morning grind over, Mann had lunch in his studio
and enjoyed his first cigar—he smoked while writing, but
limited himself to twelve cigarettes and two cigars daily.
Then he sat on the sofa and read newspapers, periodicals,
and books until 4:00, when he returned to bed for an
hour-long nap. (Once again, the children were forbidden
to make noise during this sacred hour.) At 5:00, Mann
rejoined the family for tea. Then he wrote letters, reviews,

or newspaper articles—work that could be interrupted by telephone calls or visitors—and took a walk before dinner at 7:30 or 8:00. Sometimes the family entertained guests at this time. If not, Mann and his wife would spend the evening reading or playing gramophone records before retiring to their separate bedrooms at midnight.

Karl Marx (1818-1883)

Marx arrived in London as a political exile in 1849, expecting to stay in the city for a few months at most; instead, he ended up living there until his death in 1883. His first few years in London were marked by dire poverty and personal tragedy—his family was forced to live in squalid conditions, and by 1855 three of his six children had died. Isaiah Berlin describes Marx's habits during this time:

> His mode of living consisted of daily visits to the British [Museum] reading-room, where he normally remained from nine in the morning until it closed at seven; this was followed by long hours of work at night, accompanied by ceaseless smoking, which from a luxury had become an indispensable anodyne; this affected his health permanently and he became liable to frequent attacks of a disease of the liver sometimes accompanied by boils and an inflammation of the eyes, which interfered with his work, exhausted and irritated him, and interrupted

his never certain means of livelihood. "I am plagued like Job, though not so God-fearing," he wrote in 1858.

Marx was, by 1858, already several years into *Das Kapital*, the massive work of political economy that would occupy the rest of his life. He never had a regular job. "I must pursue my goal through thick and thin and I must not allow bourgeois society to turn me into a money-making machine," he wrote in 1859. (In fact, he later applied for a post as a railway clerk, but was rejected because of his illegible handwriting.) Instead, Marx relied on his friend and collaborator Friedrich Engels to send him regular handouts, which Engels pilfered from the petty-cash box of his father's textile firm—and which Marx promptly misspent, having no money-management skills whatsoever. "I don't suppose anyone has ever written about 'money' when so short of the stuff," he noted. Meanwhile, his boils would get so bad that he "could neither sit nor walk nor remain upright," as one biographer put it. In the end, it took Marx two decades of daily suffering to complete the first volume of *Das Kapital*—and he died before he could finish the remaining two volumes. Yet he had only one regret. "You know that I have sacrificed my whole fortune to the revolutionary struggle," he wrote to a fellow political activist in 1866. "I do not regret it. On the contrary. Had I my career to start again, I should do the same. But I would not marry. As far as lies in my power I intend to save my daughter from the reefs on which her mother's life has been wrecked."

Sigmund Freud (1856-1939)

"I cannot imagine life without work as really comfortable," Freud wrote to a friend in 1910. With his wife, Martha, to efficiently manage the household—she laid out Freud's clothes, chose his handkerchiefs, and even put toothpaste on his toothbrush—the founder of psychoanalysis was able to maintain a single-minded devotion to his work throughout his long career. Freud rose each day by 7:00, ate breakfast, and had his beard trimmed by a barber who made a daily house call for this purpose. Then he saw analytic patients from 8:00 until noon. Dinner, the principal meal of the day, was served promptly at 1:00. Freud was not a gourmet—he disliked wine and chicken, and preferred solid middle-class fare like boiled or roast beef—but he enjoyed his food and ate with quiet concentration. Although normally a genial host, Freud could be so absorbed by his thoughts during the meal that his silence sometimes discomfited guests, who would struggle to carry a conversation with the other members of the family.

After dinner, Freud went for a walk around Vienna's Ringstrasse. This was not a leisurely stroll, however; his son, Martin, recalled, "My father marched at terrific speed." Along the way he would often purchase cigars and collect or deliver proofs to his publisher. At 3:00 there were consultations, followed by more analytic patients, until 9:00 at night. Then the family ate supper, and Freud would play a game of cards with his sister-in-law or go for a walk with his wife or one of his daughters, sometimes stopping at a café to read the papers. The remainder of the evenings was spent in his study, reading, writing, and doing editorial chores for psychoanalytical journals, until 1:00 A.M. or later.

Freud's long workdays were mitigated by two luxuries. First, there were his beloved cigars, which he smoked continually, going through as many as twenty a day from his mid-twenties until near the end of his life, despite several warnings from doctors and the increasingly dire health problems that dogged him throughout his later years. (When his seventeen-year-old nephew once refused a cigarette, Freud told him, "My boy, smoking is one of the greatest and cheapest enjoyments in life, and if you decide in advance not to smoke, I can only feel sorry for you.") Equally important, no doubt, were the family's annual three-month summer vacations, which they spent in a spa or hotel in the mountains, going on hikes, gathering mushrooms and strawberries, and fishing.

Carl Jung (1875-1961)

In 1922, Jung bought a parcel of land near the small village of Bollingen, Switzerland, and began construction on a simple two-story stone house along the shore of the upper basin of Lake Zurich. Over the next dozen years he modified and expanded the Bollingen Tower, as it became known, adding a pair of smaller auxiliary towers and a walled-in courtyard with a large outdoor fire pit. Even with these additions, it remained a primitive dwelling. No floorboards or carpets covered the uneven stone floor. There was no electricity and no telephone. Heat came from

Carl Jung, Bollingen Tower, circa 1960

chopped wood, cooking was done on an oil stove, and the only artificial light came from oil lamps. Water had to be brought up from the lake and boiled (eventually, a hand pump was installed). "If a man of the sixteenth century were to move into the house, only the kerosene lamps and the matches would be new to him," Jung wrote; "otherwise, he would know his way about without difficulty."

Throughout the 1930s, Jung used Bollingen Tower as a retreat from city life, where he led a workaholic's existence, seeing patients for eight or nine hours a day and delivering frequent lectures and seminars. As a result, nearly all Jung's writing was done on holidays. (And although he had many patients who relied on him, Jung was not shy about taking time off; "I've realized that somebody who's tired and needs a rest, and goes on working all the same is a fool," he said.)

At Bollingen, Jung rose at 7:00 A.M.; said good morning to his saucepans, pots, and frying pans; and "spent a long time preparing breakfast, which usually consisted of coffee, salami, fruits, bread and butter," the biographer Ronald Hayman notes. He generally set aside two hours in the morning for concentrated writing. The rest of his day would be spent painting or meditating in his private study, going for long walks in the hills, receiving visitors, and replying to the never-ending stream of letters that arrived each day. At 2:00 or 3:00 he took tea; in the evening he enjoyed preparing a large meal, often preceded by an aperitif, which he called a "sun-downer." Bedtime was at 10:00. "At Bollingen I am in the midst of my true life, I am most deeply myself," Jung wrote. ". . . I have done without electricity, and tend the fireplace and stove myself. Evenings, I light the old lamps. There is no running water, I pump the water from the well. I chop the wood and cook the food. These simple acts make man simple; and how difficult it is to be simple!"

Gustav Mahler (1860-1911)

Although Mahler is now recognized as one of the leading composers of the late nineteenth and early twentieth centuries, in his own lifetime he was better known as a conductor. Indeed, for most of his life, composing was a part-time activity. The mature symphonies of Mahler's middle period were conceived during his summers away from a demanding post as the director of the Vienna Court Opera. He spent those summers at a villa at Maiernigg, on the Wörthersee lake in southern Austria. An excellent record of his habits there comes from the memoirs of his wife, Alma, a woman nineteen years his junior. They met in November 1901, married four months later, and traveled to the villa together the next summer. Alma was pregnant with their first child; Mahler brought along the sketches for his Fifth Symphony, a breakthrough work that encompasses a vast swath of moods, from the opening funeral march to an achingly beautiful fourth movement dedicated to his new bride.

But if Mahler's work pointed to a passionate, tempestuous inner life, his habits at Maiernigg displayed the opposite. The composer's life at the villa, Alma discovered, "was stripped of all dross, almost inhuman in its purity." He woke at 6:00 or 6:30 A.M. and immediately rang for the cook to prepare his breakfast: freshly ground coffee, milk, diet bread, butter, and jam, which the cook carried to Mahler's stone composing hut in the woods. (Mahler could not bear to see or speak to anyone before settling down to work in the morning, so the cook had to take a steep, slippery path to the hut rather than the main walkway, in order not to risk running into him.) Upon arriving at the hut, Mahler would light a small spirit stove—"he nearly always burned his fingers," Alma noted, "not so much from clumsiness as from a dreamy absence of mind"—heat the milk for his coffee, and eat his breakfast on a bench outside. Then he shut himself inside to work. Meanwhile, Alma's job was to make sure that no sound carried to the hut during Mahler's working hours. She refrained from playing the piano, and promised the neighbors opera tickets if they would keep their dogs locked up.

Mahler worked until midday, then silently returned to his room, changed clothes, and walked down to the lake for a swim. Once he was in the water, he would whistle for his wife to join him on the beach. Mahler liked to lie in the sun until he was dry, then jump into the water again, often repeating this four or five times, which left him feeling invigorated and ready for lunch at home. The meal was, to Mahler's preference, light, simple, thoroughly cooked, and minimally seasoned. "Its purpose was to satisfy without tempting the appetite or causing any sensation of heaviness," wrote Alma, to whom it seemed "an invalid's diet."

Gustav and Alma Mahler, near their summer residence, 1909

After lunch, Mahler would drag Alma on a three- or four-hour-long walk along the shore, stopping occasionally to jot down ideas in his notebook, beating time in the air with his pencil. These composing breaks would sometimes last for an hour or longer, during which time Alma would sit on a branch or in the grass, not daring to look at her husband. "If his inspiration pleased him he smiled back at me," she recalled. "He knew that nothing in the world was a greater joy to me." In reality, Alma was not quite so sanguine about her new station as dutiful wife to a moody, solitary artist. (Prior to their marriage, she had been a promising composer in her own right, but Mahler had made her quit, saying that there could be only one composer in the family.) As she wrote in her diary that July, "There's such a struggle going on in me! And a miserable longing for someone who thinks OF ME, who helps me to find MYSELF! I've sunk to the level of a housekeeper!"

Mahler, for his part, seemed unaware of his wife's inner turmoil, or else chose to ignore it. By the autumn he had largely completed the Fifth, and for the next several summers he would continue the exact same lifestyle, composing his Sixth, Seventh, and Eighth symphonies at Maiernigg. As long as the work was going well, he was content. He wrote to a colleague, "You know that all I desire and demand of life is to feel an urge to work!"

Richard Strauss (1864–1949)

Strauss's creative process was methodical and angst-free; he compared his need to compose to a cow giving milk.

Even in late 1892, when Strauss left Germany to recover from bouts of pleurisy and bronchitis in a warmer climate, he quickly established a regular work schedule. He wrote home from a hotel in Egypt:

> My day's work is very simple; I get up at 8 o'clock, have a bath and breakfast; 3 eggs, tea, "Eingemachtes" [homemade jam]; then I go for a stroll for half an hour by the Nile in the palm grove of the hotel, and work from 10 till 1; the orchestration of the first Act goes forward slowly but surely. At 1 o'clock I have lunch, then read my Schopenhauer or play Bezique with Mrs. Conze for a piastre stake. From 3 till 4 I work on; at 4 o'clock tea, and after that I go for a walk until 6 when I do my duty in admiring the usual sunset. At 6 o'clock it gets cool and dark; then I write letters or work a bit more until 7. At 7 dinner, after which I chat and smoke (8–12 a day), at half past 9 I go to my room, read for half an hour and put out the light at ten. So it goes on day after day.

Henri Matisse (1869-1954)

"Basically, I enjoy everything: I am never bored," Matisse told a visitor in 1941, during a tour of his studio in the south of France. After showing his guest his working space, his cages full of exotic birds, and his conservatory stocked with tropical plants, giant pumpkins, and Chinese statuettes, Matisse talked about his work habits.

Henri Matisse in his studio at Villa Le Rêve, near Vence, the south of France, 1944

Do you understand now why I am never bored? For over fifty years I have not stopped working for an instant. From nine o'clock to noon, first sitting. I have lunch. Then I have a little nap and take up my brushes again at two in the afternoon until the evening. You won't believe me. On Sundays, I have to tell all sorts of tales to the models. I promise them that it's the last time I will ever beg them to come and pose on that day. Naturally I pay them double. Finally, when I sense that they are not convinced, I promise them a day off during the week. "But Monsieur Matisse," one of them answered me, "this has been going on for months and I have never had one afternoon off." Poor things! They don't understand. Nevertheless I can't sacrifice my Sundays for them merely because they have boyfriends.

Joan Miró (1893–1983)

Miró always maintained a rigidly inflexible daily routine—both because he disliked being distracted from his work, and because he feared slipping back into the severe depression that had afflicted him as a young man, before he discovered painting. To help prevent a relapse, his routine always included vigorous exercise—boxing in Paris; jumping rope and Swedish gymnastics at a Barcelona gym; and running on the beach and swimming at Mont-roig, a seaside village where his family owned a farmhouse, to which Miró returned nearly every summer to escape city life and recharge his creative energies. In *Miró: The Life of a Passion*, Lluís Permanyer describes the artist's routine in the early 1930s, when he was living in Barcelona with his wife and young daughter:

[A]t six o'clock he got up, washed and had coffee and a few slices of bread for breakfast; at seven he went into the studio and worked non-stop until twelve, when he stopped to do an hour of energetic exercise, like boxing or running; at one o'clock he sat down for a frugal but well-prepared lunch, which he finished off with a coffee and three cigarettes, neither more nor less; then he practised his "Mediterranean

Joan Miró in his Barcelona studio, 1953

yoga," a nap, but for just five minutes; at two he would receive a friend, deal with business matters or write letters; at three he returned to the studio, where he stayed until dinner time at eight o'clock; after dinner he would read for a while or listen to music.

Miró hated for this routine to be interrupted by social or cultural events. As he told an American journalist, "Merde! I absolutely detest all openings and parties! They're commercial, political, and everybody talks too much. They get on my tits!"

Gertrude Stein (1874-1946)

After the outbreak of World War II, Stein and her life-long partner, Alice B. Toklas, fled Paris for a country home in Ain, on the eastern edge of France. Stein had long depended on Toklas to take care of their living arrangements; in Ain, as Janet Malcolm writes in *Two Lives: Gertrude and Alice*, Toklas "managed the practical details of Stein's life almost to the point of parody." A 1934 *New Yorker* piece by Janet Flanner, James Thurber, and Harold Ross described their lifestyle:

Miss Stein gets up every morning about ten and drinks some coffee, against her will. She's always been nervous about becoming nervous and she thought coffee would make her nervous, but her doctor prescribed it. Miss Toklas, her companion, gets up at six and starts dusting and fussing around. . . . Every morning Miss Toklas bathes and combs their French poodle, Basket, and brushes its teeth. It has its own toothbrush.

Miss Stein has an outsize bathtub that was especially made for her. A staircase had to be taken out to install it. After her bath she puts on a huge wool

Gertrude Stein, Alice B. Toklas, and their poodle on the doorstep of their house in southern France, 1944

bathrobe and writes for a while, but she prefers to write outdoors, after she gets dressed. Especially in the Ain country, because there are rocks and cows there. Miss Stein likes to look at rocks and cows in the intervals of her writing. The two ladies drive around in their Ford till they come to a good spot. Then Miss Stein gets out and sits on a campstool with pencil and pad, and Miss Toklas fearlessly switches a cow into her line of vision. If the cow doesn't seem to fit in with Miss Stein's mood, the ladies get into the car and drive on to another cow. When the great lady has an inspiration, she writes quickly, for about fifteen minutes. But often she just sits there, looking at cows and not turning a wheel.

In *Everybody's Autobiography,* Stein confirmed that she had never been able to write much more than half an hour a day—but added, "If you write a half hour a day it makes a lot of writing year by year. To be sure all day and every day you are waiting around to write that half hour a day." Stein and Toklas had lunch at about noon and ate an early, light supper. Toklas went to bed early, too, but Stein liked to stay up arguing and gossiping with visiting friends—"I never go to sleep when I go to bed I always fool around in the evening," she wrote. After her guests finally left, Stein would go wake Toklas, and they would talk over the entire day before both going to sleep.

Ernest Hemingway (1899-1961)

Throughout his adult life Hemingway rose early, at 5:30 or 6:00, woken by the first light of day. This was true even when he had been up late drinking the night before; his son Gregory recalled that the author seemed immune to hangovers: "My father would always look great, as if he'd slept a baby's sleep in a soundproof room with his eyes covered by black patches." In a 1958 interview with *The Paris Review,* Hemingway explained the importance of those early-morning hours:

When I am working on a book or a story I write every morning as soon after first light as possible. There is no one to disturb you and it is cool or cold and you come to your work and warm as you write. You read what you have written and, as you always stop when you know what is going to happen next, you go on from there. You write until you come to a place where you still have your juice and know what will happen next and you stop and try to live through until the next day when you hit it again. You have started at six in the morning, say, and may go on until noon or be through before that. When you stop you are as empty, and at the same time never empty but filling, as when you have made love to someone you love. Nothing can hurt you, nothing can happen, nothing means anything until the next day when you do it again. It is the wait until that next day that is hard to get through.

Contrary to popular lore, Hemingway did not begin each session by sharpening twenty number-two pencils— "I don't think I ever owned twenty pencils at one time," he told *The Paris Review*—but he did have his share of writing idiosyncrasies. He wrote standing up, facing a chest-high bookshelf with a typewriter on top, and on top of that a wooden reading board. First drafts were composed in pencil on onionskin typewriter paper laid slantwise across the board; when the work was going well, Hemingway would remove the board and shift to the typewriter. He tracked his daily word output on a chart—"so as not to kid myself," he said. When the writing wasn't going well, he would often knock off the fiction and answer letters, which gave him a welcome break from "the awful responsibility of writing"—or, as he sometimes called it, "the responsibility of awful writing."

Henry Miller (1891-1980)

As a young novelist, Miller frequently wrote from midnight until dawn—until he realized that he was really a morning person. Living in Paris in the early 1930s, Miller shifted his writing time, working from breakfast to lunch, taking a nap, then writing again through the afternoon and sometimes into the night. As he got older, though, he found that anything after noon was unnecessary and even counterproductive. As he told one interviewer, "I don't believe in draining the reservoir, do you see? I believe in getting up from the typewriter, away from it, while I still have things to say." Two or three hours in the morning were enough for him, although he stressed the importance of keeping regular hours in order to cultivate a daily creative rhythm. "I know that to sustain these true moments of insight one has to be highly disciplined, lead a disciplined life," he said.

F. Scott Fitzgerald (1896-1940)

At the outset of his literary career, Fitzgerald demonstrated remarkable self-discipline. When he enlisted in the army in 1917 and was sent to training camp in Fort

Leavenworth, Kansas, the barely twenty-one-year-old Princeton dropout composed a 120,000-word novel in only three months. He initially worked during evening study periods, scribbling on a pad of paper concealed behind a copy of *Small Problems for Infantry*; when that ruse was detected, Fitzgerald switched to the weekends, writing in the officer's club from 1:00 P.M. to midnight on Saturdays and from 6:00 A.M. to 6:00 P.M. on Sundays. By early 1918, he had mailed off the manuscript that would eventually become, with major revisions, *This Side of Paradise*.

But in his post-military writing life, Fitzgerald always had trouble sticking to a regular schedule. Living in Paris in 1925, he generally rose at 11:00 A.M. and tried to start writing at 5:00 P.M., working on and off until 3:30 in the morning. In reality, however, many of his nights were spent on the town, making the rounds of the cafés with Zelda. The real writing usually happened in brief bursts of concentrated activity, during which he could manage seven thousand or eight thousand words in one session. This method worked pretty well for short stories, which Fitzgerald preferred to compose in a spontaneous manner. "Stories are best written in either one jump or three, according to the length," he once explained. "The three-jump story should be done in three successive days, then a day or so for revise and off she goes."

Novels were trickier, especially since Fitzgerald increasingly believed that alcohol was essential to his creative process. (He preferred straight gin—it worked fast and was, he thought, difficult to detect on one's breath.) When he was working on *Tender Is the Night,* Fitzgerald tried to reserve a portion of each day for sober composition. But he went on regular binges and later admitted to his editor that alcohol had interfered with the novel. "It has become increasingly plain to me that the very excellent organization of a long book or the finest perceptions and judgment in time of revision do not go well with liquor," he wrote.

William Faulkner (1897-1962)

Faulkner usually wrote best in the morning, although throughout his life he was able to adapt to various schedules as necessary. He wrote *As I Lay Dying* in the afternoons before clocking in on the night shift as a supervisor at a university power plant. He found the nocturnal schedule easy enough to manage: he would sleep in the morning for a few hours, write all afternoon, visit his mother for coffee on the way to work, and take catnaps throughout his undemanding shift.

This was 1929. In the summer of 1930, the Faulkners purchased a large, dilapidated family estate, and Faulkner quit his job in order to repair the house and grounds. Then he would wake early, eat breakfast, and write at his desk all morning. (Faulkner liked to work in the library, and since the library door had no lock, he would remove the doorknob and take it with him.) After a noon lunch, he would continue repairs on the house and take a long walk or go horseback riding. In the evenings Faulkner and his wife would relax on the porch with a bottle of whiskey.

As for the popular conception that Faulkner drank while writing, it's unclear whether this is true. Several of his friends and acquaintances reported the habit, but his daughter emphatically denied it, insisting that he "always wrote when sober, and would drink afterwards." In any case, he did not seem to need an inducement for his creativity. During his most fertile years, from the late 1920s through the early '40s, Faulkner worked at an astonishing pace, often completing three thousand words a day and occasionally twice that amount. (He once wrote to his mother that he had managed ten thousand words in one day, working between 10:00 A.M. and midnight—a personal record.) "I write when the spirit moves me," Faulkner said, "and the spirit moves me every day."

Arthur Miller (1915-2005)

"I wish I had a routine for writing," Miller told an interviewer in 1999. "I get up in the morning and I go out to my studio and I write. And then I tear it up! That's the routine, really. Then, occasionally, something sticks. And then I follow that. The only image I can think of is a man walking around with an iron rod in his hand during a lightning storm."

Benjamin Britten (1913-1976)

The English composer and conductor hated the Romantic cliché of the creative artist waiting for inspiration to strike. He said in a 1967 television interview:

> That isn't the way I work. I like working to an exact timetable. I often thank my stars that I had a rather conventional upbringing, that I went to a rather strict school where one was made to work. And I can without much difficulty sit down at nine o'clock in the morning and work straight through the morning until lunchtime, then in the afternoon letters—or, rather more important, is that I go for a walk, where I plan out what I'm going to write in the next period at my desk. I then come back. After tea, up to my studio and work through until about eight o'clock. After dinner I usually find I'm too sleepy to do much more than read a little bit, and then go to bed rather early.

In the morning Britten had a cold bath; in the evening, a hot one. In the summer he liked to swim, and he would play tennis on the weekends when he could. Around the house, he was hopeless. Britten's longtime partner and collaborator, Peter Pears, remembers, "He could make a cup of tea, boil an egg and wash up, but not much more. If he made his bed, he usually made a mess of it." Britten's life was his work—a fact that alienated some of his colleagues over the years. "Functioning as a composer was his whole world," Donald Mitchell recalled. "The creativity had to come first. . . . Everyone, including himself, had to be sacrificed to the creative act."

Ann Beattie (b. 1947)

Beattie works best at night. "I really believe in day people and night people," she told an interviewer in 1980.

> I really think people's bodies are on different clocks. I even feel now like I just woke up and I've been awake for three or four hours. And I'll feel this way until seven o'clock tonight when I'll start to pick up and then by nine it will be O.K. to start writing. My favorite hours are from 12:00 to 3:00 A.M. for writing.

She doesn't write every night, however. "I really don't adhere to schedules at all, and don't have the slightest desire to do that," she said. "The times that I've tried that, when I have been in a slump and I try to get out of it by saying, 'Come on, Ann, sit down at that typewriter,' I've gotten in a worse slump. It's better if I just let it ride." As a result, she often won't write anything for months. "I've learned I can't force it," she said. But that doesn't mean that she is able to relax and enjoy herself during these fallow periods; rather, she says it's like having an almost permanent case of writer's block. As she told an interviewer in 1998, "I certainly am a moody and, I would say, not very happy person."

Günter Grass (b. 1927)

Asked if he writes during the day or at night, Grass seemed to shudder at the latter notion: "Never, never at night. I don't believe in writing at night because it comes too easily. When I read it in the morning it's not good. I need daylight to begin. Between nine and ten o'clock I have a long breakfast with reading and music. After breakfast I work, and then take a break for coffee in the afternoon. I start again and finish at seven o'clock in the evening."

Tom Stoppard (b. 1937)

The playwright has struggled with chronic disorganization and procrastination throughout his career. He once noted that the only thing that really got him to write was fear—he had to get "frightened enough to discipline myself to the typewriter for successive bouts." Then he would sit up all night writing and smoking, usually working in the kitchen while the rest of the household was asleep. His biographer, Ira Nadel, notes that Stoppard's smoking habits were unusual as well: "An inveterate chain-smoker, he was notorious for stubbing out a cigarette after one or two puffs and then lighting another. This, he calculated, was equivalent to smoking with a very long filter."

At various times, Stoppard attempted to reform his "ineffectual inefficiency" as a writer; in the early 1980s he even succeeded in chaining himself to the desk from roughly 10:00 A.M. to 5:00 P.M. daily. But he gradually slipped back into old habits. In 1997, he told a reporter that he generally worked from midday to midnight, adding, "I never work in the mornings unless I'm in real trouble."

Haruki Murakami (b. 1949)

When he is writing a novel, Murakami wakes at 4:00 A.M. and works for five to six hours straight. In the afternoons he runs or swims (or does both), runs errands, reads, and listens to music; bedtime is 9:00. "I keep to this routine every day without variation," he told *The Paris Review* in 2004. "The repetition itself becomes the important thing; it's a form of mesmerism. I mesmerize myself to reach a deeper state of mind."

Murakami has said that maintaining this repetition for the time required to complete a novel takes more than mental discipline: "Physical strength is as necessary as artistic sensitivity." When he first hung out his shingle as a professional writer, in 1981, after several years running a small jazz club in Tokyo, he discovered that the sedentary lifestyle caused him to gain weight rapidly; he was also smoking as many as sixty cigarettes a day. He soon resolved to change his habits completely, moving with his wife to a rural area, quitting smoking, drinking less, and eating a diet of mostly vegetables and fish. He also started running daily, a habit he has kept up for more than a quarter century.

The one drawback to this self-made schedule, Murakami admitted in a 2008 essay, is that it doesn't allow for much of a social life. "People are offended when you repeatedly turn down their invitations," he wrote. But he decided that the indispensable relationship in his life was with his readers. "My readers would welcome whatever life style I chose, as long as I made sure each new work was an improvement over the last. And shouldn't that be my duty—and my top priority—as a novelist?"

Toni Morrison (b. 1931)

"I am not able to write regularly," Morrison told *The Paris Review* in 1993. "I have never been able to do that—mostly because I have always had a nine-to-five job. I had to write either in between those hours, hurriedly, or spend a lot of weekend and predawn time." Indeed, for much of her writing career, Morrison not only worked a day job—as an editor at Random House—but taught university literature courses and raised her two sons as a single parent. "It does seem hectic," she admitted in 1977.

But the important thing is that I don't do anything else. I avoid the social life normally associated with publishing. I don't go to the cocktail parties, I don't give or go to dinner parties. I need that time in the evening because I can do a tremendous amount of work then. And I can concentrate. When I sit down to write I never brood. I have so many other things to do, with my children and teaching, that I can't afford it. I brood, thinking of ideas, in the automobile when I'm driving to work or in the subway or when I'm mowing the lawn. By the time I get to the paper something's there—I can produce.

Morrison's writing hours have varied over the years. In interviews in the 1970s and '80s, she frequently mentions working on her fiction in the evenings. But by the '90s, she had switched to the early morning hours, saying, "I am not very bright or very witty or very inventive after the sun goes down." For the morning writing, her ritual is to rise around 5:00, make coffee, and "watch the light come." This last part is crucial. "Writers all devise ways to approach that place where they expect to make the contact, where they become the conduit, or where they engage in this mysterious process," Morrison said. "For me, light is the signal in the transaction. It's not being *in* the light, it's being there *before it arrives*. It enables me, in some sense."

Joyce Carol Oates (b. 1938)

The famously prolific American writer—Oates has published more than fifty novels, thirty-six collections of short stories, and dozens of volumes of poetry, drama, and essays—generally writes from 8:00 or 8:30 in the morning until 1:00 P.M. Then she eats lunch and allows herself an afternoon break before resuming work from 4:00 P.M. until dinner at around 7:00. Sometimes she will continue writing after dinner, but more often she reads in the evening. Given the number of hours she spends at the desk, Oates has pointed out, her productivity is not really so remarkable. "I write and write and write, and rewrite, and even if I retain only a single page from a full day's work, it *is* a single page, and these pages add up," she told one interviewer. "As a result I have acquired the reputation over the years of being prolix when in fact I am measured against people who simply don't work as hard or as long." This doesn't mean that she always finds the work pleasant or easy; the first several weeks of a new novel, Oates has said, are particularly difficult and demoralizing: "Getting the first draft finished is like pushing a peanut with your nose across a very dirty floor."

Chuck Close (b. 1940)

"In an ideal world, I would work six hours a day, three hours in the morning and three hours in the afternoon," Close said recently.

> That's what I always liked to do. Especially since my kids were born. I used to work at night, but when my kids were born I couldn't just work at night and sleep during the day. So that's when I started having a kind of regular, nine-to-five work schedule. And if I work more than three hours at a time, I really start screwing up. So the idea is to work for three hours, break for lunch, go back and work for three hours, and then, you know, break. Sometimes I could go

back and work in the evening, but basically it was counterproductive. At a certain point, I'd start making enough mistakes that I would spend the next day trying to correct them.

Unfortunately, Close says, his life now has so many obligations that he is often unable to stick to this routine. (He tries to schedule all meetings and phone calls for after 4:00 P.M., but has found that this is not always possible.) When he does find the time to work, he never lacks for ideas. "Inspiration is for amateurs," Close says. "The rest of us just show up and get to work." While he paints, he likes to have the TV or the radio playing in the background—particularly if there's a juicy political scandal happening. "My finest hours were Watergate, Iran-Contra, the impeachment," he says. The constant chatter can be distracting, he admits, but he claims that this is actually a good thing: "I like a certain amount of distraction. It keeps me from being anxious. It keeps things at a little bit more of an arm's length."

Francine Prose (b. 1947)

The American author has found that literary success has made literary productivity increasingly difficult. She writes:

> Back in the day, when my kids were little and I lived in the country and I was an unknown novelist, I had a schedule so regular that it was practically Pavlov-

ian, and I loved it. The school bus came, I started to write. The school bus returned, I stopped. Now that I'm in the city and my kids are grown and the world, it seems, will pay me to do anything BUT write (or in any case para-literary activities often seem more lucrative and frequently more seductive than actual writing) my routine is more haphazard. I write whenever I am able, for a few days or a week or a month if I can get the time. I sneak away to the country and work on a computer that's not connected to the Internet and count on the world to go away long enough for me to get a few words down on paper, whenever and however I can. When the writing is going well, I can work all day. When it's not, I spend a lot of time gardening and standing in front of the refrigerator.

John Adams (b. 1947)

"My experience has been that most really serious creative people I know have very, very routine and not particularly glamorous work habits," Adams said in a recent interview. "Because creativity, particularly the kind of work I do—which is writing large-scale pieces, either symphonic music or opera music—is just, it's very labor-intensive. And it's something that you can't do with an assistant. You have to do it all by yourself." Adams works most days in a studio in his Berkeley, California, home. (He keeps another, mirror-image studio in a remote wooded location along the California coast, where he goes to work for short periods.) "When I'm home, I get up in the morning and I have a very active dog, so I take the dog up into the high mountains behind where we live," he says. Then he heads into the studio and works from 9:00 A.M. until 4:00 or 5:00 in the afternoon, taking breaks to go downstairs and make "endless cups of green tea." Otherwise, Adams says that he doesn't have any particular creative rituals or superstitions: "I find basically that if I do things regularly, I don't have writer's block or come into terrible crises."

This doesn't mean, however, that all his studio time is spent in concentrated creative work. "I confess that I'm not as Zen disciplined or as pure as I'd like," he says. "Often after an hour of working I'll yield to the temptation to read my e-mail or things like that. The problem is that you do get run out of concentration energy and sometimes you just want to take a mental break. But if you get tangled up into some complicated communication with somebody, the next thing you know you look up and you've lost forty-five minutes of time." In the evening, Adams generally tries to switch off. He doesn't listen to a lot of music; after spending the day composing, he's usually had enough. "At the end of the day I'm more apt to want to cook a nice meal or read a book or watch a movie with my wife," he says.

Although he maintains a regular working schedule, Adams also tries not to overplan his musical life. "I actually really demand from myself a sort of inordinate amount of unstructured freedom," he says. "I don't want to know what I'm doing the next year or even the next week. I somehow have this feeling that to keep the spontaneity from my creative work fresh I need to be in a state of rather shocking irresponsibility." Of course he has to make commitments and set premiere dates and things of that nature. But, he says, "I also try to keep a sort of random freedom about my daily life so that I can be open for ideas when they come."

Steve Reich (b. 1936)

"I'm not really a morning person," the American composer said recently. "I would say, if you look at everything I've ever written, ninety-five percent of it would have been written between twelve noon and twelve midnight." Reich uses the hours before noon to exercise, pray, eat breakfast, and make business phone calls to London, where his European agent is based. Then, once he settles down in front of the piano or the computer, he'll aim for a few good chunks of concentrated work over the next twelve hours. "If I can get in a couple hours of work, then I just have to have a cup of tea, or I have to run an errand to get a little bit of a break," he says. "And then I come back. But those can be very fruitful pauses, especially if there's a little problem that comes up. The best thing to do is to just leave it and put your mind somewhere else, and not always but often the solution to that problem will bubble up spontaneously. Or at least a possible solution, which will either prove to be true or false." Reich doesn't believe in waiting for inspiration to strike, but he does believe that certain pieces are more inspired than others—and that, with continual work, you can look forward to hitting these patches of inspiration from time to time. "There are no rules," he says. "One has to be open to the reality—and it's a very wonderful reality—that the next piece is going to hold some surprises for you."

Nicholson Baker (b. 1957)

Baker's novels display a near-obsessive interest in the mundane details of daily life, so it's not surprising that, in his own life, the author pays a lot of attention to his writing schedule and habits. "What I've found with daily routines," he said recently, "is that the useful thing is to have one that feels new. It can almost be arbitrary. You know, you could say to yourself, 'From now on, I'm only going to write on the back porch in flip flops starting at four o'clock in the afternoon.' And if that feels novel and fresh, it will have a placebo effect and it will help you work. Maybe that's not completely true. But there's something to just the excitement of coming up with a slightly different routine. I find I have to do it for each book, have something different."

While he was writing his first book, *The Mezzanine,* Baker worked a series of office jobs in Boston and New York. Then his routine was to write on his lunch break, taking advantage of this "pure, blissful hour of freedom" in the middle of the day to make notes for a novel that was, appropriately, about an office drone returning to work from his lunch hour. Later, Baker worked a job outside of Boston that required a ninety-minute commute, so he bought a mini–cassette recorder and dictated his writing while he drove. Eventually he quit that job and took a couple of months, writing eight or nine hours a day, to pull all his lunch-hour and commuting notes together into a coherent novel.

For subsequent books, Baker says that he was not terribly strict about his writing schedule. "There was a lot of putting off," he admits. "I would read stuff and try to get revved up, and sometimes I wouldn't get started writing until about two-thirty in the afternoon." It took another day job to force him into more consistent habits. From 1999 until 2004, Baker and his wife found themselves running the American Newspaper Repository, a non-profit dedicated to saving a collection of newspapers that would otherwise have been destroyed (one of the subjects of Baker's 2001 nonfiction book, *Double Fold: Libraries and the Assault on Paper*). Since he was busy during the day, Baker, inspired by the example of Frances Trollope (see p. 25), resolved to write in the early mornings. Initially he tried to get up at 3:30 A.M., but "that didn't work too well" so he revised it to 4:30. "And I liked it, I liked the feeling of getting up really early," he says. "The mind is newly cleansed but it's also befuddled and you're still just plain sleepy. I found that I wrote differently then."

Baker liked the early-morning feeling so much that he has stuck with this schedule ever since—and, more recently, has developed a strategy to squeeze two mornings out of one day. He says, "A typical day for me would be that I would get up around four, four-thirty. And I write some. Make coffee sometimes, or not. I write for maybe an hour and a half. *But then I get really sleepy.* So I go back to sleep and then I wake up at around eight-thirty." After waking for the second time, Baker talks with his wife, drinks another cup of coffee, eats a peanut-butter-and-jelly sandwich, and goes back to his writing, this time focusing on "daylight kind of work," like typing up notes for a nonfiction piece, transcribing an interview, or editing what he wrote during the first morning session. He continues to work more or less all day, stopping to have lunch, walk the dog, and run errands as necessary. Occasionally, if he's feeling a lot of deadline pressure, he will write late at night as well, but he generally says good night to his wife and kids around 9:30 P.M.

B. F. Skinner (1904-1990)

The founder of behavioral psychology treated his daily writing sessions much like a laboratory experiment, conditioning himself to write every morning with a pair of self-reinforcing behaviors: he started and stopped by the buzz of a timer, and he carefully plotted the number of hours he wrote and the words he produced on a graph. In a 1963 journal entry, Skinner provided a detailed description of his routine:

> I rise sometime between 6 and 6:30 often after having heard the radio news. My breakfast, a dish of corn flakes, is on the kitchen table. Coffee is made automatically by the stove timer. I breakfast alone. At the moment, I am reading a bit every morning of Bergen and Cornelia Evans' *Contemporary American Usage*. A couple of pages every day, straight through. The morning papers (*Boston Globe, N.Y.*

Times) arrive, thrown against the wall or door of the kitchen where I breakfast. I read the *Globe,* often saving the *Times* till later.

At seven or so I go down to my study, a walnut-paneled room in our basement. My work desk is a long Scandinavian-modern table, with a set of shelves I made myself for holding the works of BFS, notebooks and outlines of the book I am working on, dictionaries, word-books, etc. On my left the big Webster's *International* on a stand, on my right an open-top file containing all current and future manuscript materials. As I sit down I turn on a special desk light. This starts a clock, which totalizes my time at my desk. Every twelve hours recorded on it, I plot a point on a cumulative curve, the slope of which shows my overall productivity. To the right of my desk is an electric organ, on which a few minutes each day I play Bach *Chorales* etc.

Later in the morning I go to my office. These days I leave just before 10 so that Debbie can ride with me to her summer school class. Later, in cooler weather, I will be walking—about 1¾ miles. In my office I open and answer mail, see people if necessary. Get away as soon as possible, usually in time for lunch at home. Afternoons are not profitably spent, working in [the] garden, swimming in our pool. Summers we often have friends in for a swim and drinks from 5 to 7 or possibly 8. Then dinner. Light reading. Little or no work. In bed by 9:30 or 10:00. I usually wake up for an hour or so during the night. I have a clip-board, paper pad and pencil (with a small flashlight attached to the board) for making notes at night. I am not an insomniac. I enjoy that nightly hour and make good use of it. I sleep alone.

By the time Skinner retired from his Harvard teaching post in 1974, that nightly hour of sleeplessness had become an integral part of his routine. His timer now rang four times a day: at midnight, 1:00 A.M., 5:00 A.M., and 7:00 A.M., for one hour of nocturnal composition in addition to his usual two hours at dawn. He followed this routine seven days a week, holidays included, until only a few days before his death in 1990.

Margaret Mead (1901-1978)

The renowned cultural anthropologist was always working; indeed, not working seemed to agitate and unsettle her. Once, during a two-week symposium, Mead learned that a certain morning session had been postponed. She was furious. "How dare they?" she asked. "Do they *realize* what use I could have made of this time? Do they know I get up at five o'clock every morning to write a thousand words before breakfast? Why did nobody have the politeness to tell me this meeting had been rescheduled?" On other occasions, Mead would schedule breakfast dates with young colleagues for 5:00 A.M. "Empty time stretches forever," she once said. "I can't bear it."

Jonathan Edwards (1703-1758)

The eighteenth-century preacher and theologian—a key figure in the Great Awakening and the author of the sermon "Sinners in the Hands of an Angry God"—spent thirteen hours a day in his study, beginning at 4:00 or 5:00 in the morning. (He noted in his diary, "I think Christ has recommended rising early in the morning, by his rising from the grave very early.") To break up these long hours of private study, Edwards engaged in daily bouts of physical activity: chopping wood in the winter, walking or horse riding when the weather was good. On his walks, he carried a pen and ink to record his thoughts. For the horseback rides, he employed a mnemonic device, described by the biographer George W. Marsden: "For each insight he wished to remember, he would pin a small piece of paper on a particular part of his clothes, which he would associate with the thought. When he returned home he would unpin these and write down each idea. At the ends of trips of several days, his clothes might be covered by quite a few of these slips of paper."

Samuel Johnson (1709-1784)

In James Boswell's *The Life of Samuel Johnson,* Johnson tells his future biographer that he "generally went abroad at four in the afternoon, and seldom came home till two in the morning." And apparently he did much of his writing upon returning home, working by candlelight while the rest of London slept—the only time, it seems, that he could avoid the city's plentiful distractions. Boswell quotes the recollections of Rev. Dr. Maxwell, a social friend of Johnson's:

> His general mode of life, during my acquaintance, seemed to be pretty uniform. About twelve o'clock I commonly visited him, and frequently found him in bed, or declaiming over his tea, which he drank very plentifully. He generally had a levee of morning visitors, chiefly men of letters . . . and sometimes learned ladies. . . . He seemed to me to be considered as a kind of publick oracle, whom every body thought they had a right to visit and consult; and doubtless they were well rewarded. I never could discover how he found time for his compositions. He declaimed all the morning, then went to dinner at a tavern, where he commonly staid late, and then drank his tea at some friend's house, over which he loitered a great while, but seldom took supper. I fancy he must have read and wrote chiefly in the night, for I can scarcely recollect that he ever refused going with me to a tavern. . . .

Johnson readily admitted that he suffered from procrastination and a lack of discipline. "My reigning sin, to which perhaps many others are appendant, is waste of time, and general sluggishness," he wrote in his diary, and he told Boswell that "idleness is a disease which must be combated." Yet, he added, he was temperamentally ill equipped for the battle: "I myself have never persisted in any plan for two days together."

James Boswell (1740-1795)

"As soon as I am awake, I remember my duty, and like a brisk mariner I give the lash to indolence and bounce up with as much vivacity as if a pretty girl, amorous and willing, were waiting for me," Boswell boasted in his journal in 1763. In fact, the great British diarist and biographer often had a terrible time getting out of bed in the morning, and frequently fell prey to the "vile habit of wasting the precious morning hours in lazy slumber." For a while he even considered trying to rig up some sort of anti-oversleeping mechanism: "I have thought of having my bed constructed in a curious fashion. I would have it so that when I pulled a cord, the middle of the bed would be immediately raised and me raised with it and gradually set up on the floor. Thus I should be gently forced into what is good for me."

Yet, at other times, Boswell seemed perfectly content to laze about in bed before confronting the day. The fullest description of his routine comes from February 1763. "My affairs are conducted with the greatest regularity and exactness," he wrote in his diary.

I move like very clock-work. At eight in the morning Molly [the maid] lights the fire, sweeps and dresses my dining-room. Then she calls me up and lets me know what o'clock it is. I lie some time in bed indulging indolence, which in that way, when the mind is easy and cheerful, is most pleasing. I then slip on my clothes loosely, easily and quickly, and come into my dining-room. I pull my bell. The maid lays a milk-white napkin upon the table and sets the things for breakfast. I then take some light amusing book and breakfast and read for an hour or more, gently pleasing both my palate and my mental taste. Breakfast over, I feel myself gay and lively. I go to the window, and am entertained with the people passing by, all intent on different schemes. To go regularly through the day would be too formal for this my journal. Besides, every day cannot be passed exactly the same way in every particular. My day is in general diversified with reading of different kinds, playing on the violin, writing, chatting with my friends. Even the taking of medicines serves to make time go on with less heaviness. I have a sort of genius for physic and always had great entertainment in observing the changes of the human body and the effects produced by diet, labour, rest, and physical operations. . . .

As I am now in tolerable health, my appetite is very good, and I eat my slender bit of dinner with great relish. I drink a great deal of tea. Between eleven and twelve my bed is warmed and I go calmly to repose. I am not at all unsatisfied with this kind of existence.

This was Boswell on one of his good days. Other mornings he woke in a foul mood, "dreary as a dromedary," convinced that "Everything is insipid or everything is dark." Or, in the middle of a good day, depression would suddenly steal upon him out of nowhere. There seemed to be little he could do to control these black moods. To comfort himself, Boswell liked to wash his feet in warm water ("It gives me a kind of tranquility") or drink a cup of green tea, which, he wrote, "comforts and enlivens without the risks attendant of spirituous liquors." And then there was his Inviolable Plan, an elaborate and somewhat portentous pep talk and statement of purpose that he wrote to himself in October 1763. The Plan is full of resolutions large and small—to avoid idleness, to remember "the dignity of human nature," to exercise regularly—as well as some moments of hard-won insight. Boswell writes, "Life has much uneasiness; that is certain. Always remember that, and it will never surprise you."

Immanuel Kant (1724-1804)

Kant's biography is unusually devoid of external events. The philosopher lived in an isolated Prussian province for his entire life, rarely venturing outside the walls of his native Königsberg and never traveling even so far as the sea, only a few hours away. A lifelong bachelor, he taught the same courses at the local university for more than forty years. His was a life of ordered regularity—which later gave rise to a portrait of the philosopher as a sort of characterless automaton. As Heinrich Heine wrote:

> The history of Kant's life is difficult to describe. For he neither had a life nor a history. He lived a mechanically ordered, almost abstract, bachelor life in a quiet out-of-the-way lane in Königsberg, an old city at the northeast border of Germany. I do not believe that the large clock of the Cathedral there

completed its task with less passion and less regularity than its fellow citizen Immanuel Kant. Getting up, drinking coffee, writing, giving lectures, eating, taking a walk, everything had its set time, and the neighbors knew precisely that the time was 3:30 P.M. when Kant stepped outside his door with his gray coat and the Spanish stick in his hand.

In actual fact, as Manfred Kuehn argues in his 2001 biography, Kant's life was not quite as abstract and passionless as Heine and others have supposed. Kant loved to socialize, and he was a gifted conversationalist and a genial host. If he failed to live a more adventurous life, it was largely due to his health: the philosopher had a congenital skeletal defect that caused him to develop an abnormally small chest, which compressed his heart and lungs and contributed to a generally delicate constitution. In order to prolong his life with the condition—and in an effort to quell the mental anguish caused by his lifelong hypochondria—Kant adopted what he called "a certain uniformity in the way of living and in the matters about which I employ my mind."

As for the extreme fixity of this regimen, this did not develop until the philosopher reached his fortieth birthday, and then it was an expression of his unique views on human character. Character, for Kant, is a rationally chosen way of organizing one's life, based on years of varied experience—indeed, he believed that one does not really develop a character until age forty. And at the core of one's character, he thought, were maxims—a handful of essential rules for living that, once formulated, should be followed for the rest of one's life. Alas, we do not have a written list of Kant's personal maxims. But it is clear that he resolved to transform the "certain uniformity" of his lifestyle from a mere habit into a moral principle. Thus, before his fortieth birthday, Kant would sometimes stay out until midnight playing cards; after forty, he stuck to his daily routine without exception.

This routine was as follows: Kant rose at 5:00 A.M., after being woken by his longtime servant, a retired soldier under explicit orders not to let the master oversleep. Then he drank one or two cups of weak tea and smoked his pipe. According to Kuehn, "Kant had formulated the maxim for himself that he would smoke only one pipe, but it is reported that the bowls of his pipes increased considerably in size as the years went on." After this period of meditation, Kant prepared his day's lectures and did some writing. Lectures began at 7:00 A.M. and lasted until 11:00. His academic duties discharged, Kant would go to a restaurant or a pub for lunch, his only real meal of the day. He did not limit his dining company to his fellow academics but enjoyed mixing with townspeople from a variety of backgrounds. As for the meal itself, he preferred simple fare, with the meat well done, accompanied by good wine. Lunch might go until as late as 3:00, after which Kant took his famous walk and visited his closest friend, Joseph Green. They would converse until 7:00 on weekdays (9:00 on weekends, perhaps joined by another friend). Returning home, Kant would do some more work and read before going to bed precisely at 10:00.

William James (1842-1910)

In April 1870, a twenty-eight-year-old James made a cautionary note to himself in his diary. "Recollect," he wrote, "that only when habits of order are formed can we advance to really interesting fields of action—and consequently accumulate grain on grain of wilful choice like a very miser—never forgetting how one link dropped undoes an indefinite number." The importance of forming such "habits of order" later became one of James's great subjects as a psychologist. In one of the lectures he delivered to teachers in Cambridge, Massachusetts, in 1892—and eventually incorporated into his book *Psychology: A Briefer Course*—James argued that the "great thing" in education is to "make our nervous system our ally instead of our enemy."

> The more of the details of our daily life we can hand over to the effortless custody of automatism, the more our higher powers of mind will be set free for their own proper work. There is no more miserable human being than one in whom nothing is habitual but indecision, and for whom the lighting of every cigar, the drinking of every cup, the time of rising and going to bed every day, and the beginning of every bit of work, are subjects of express volitional deliberation.

James was writing from personal experience—the hypothetical sufferer is, in fact, a thinly disguised description of himself. For James kept no regular schedule, was chronically indecisive, and lived a disorderly, unsettled life. As Robert D. Richardson wrote in his 2006 biography, "James on habit, then, is not the smug advice of some martinet, but the too-late-learned too-little-self-knowing, pathetically earnest, hard-won crumbs of practical advice offered by a man who really had no habits—or who lacked the habits he most needed, having only the habit of having no habits—and whose life was itself a 'buzzing blooming confusion' that was never really under control."

Nevertheless, we can summarize a few of James's tendencies. He drank moderately and would have a cocktail before dinner. He stopped smoking and drinking coffee in his mid-thirties, although he would cheat with the occasional cigar. He suffered from insomnia, particularly when he was deep into a writing project, and beginning in the 1880s he used chloroform to put himself to sleep. Before bed, if his eyes weren't too tired, he would sit up and read until 11:00 or midnight, which, he found, "very much enlarges the day." In his later years, he took a nap every afternoon from 2:00 to 3:00. He procrastinated. As he told one of his classes, "I know a person who will poke the fire, set chairs straight, pick dust specks from the floor, arrange his table, snatch up a newspaper, take down any book which catches his eye, trim his nails, waste the morning anyhow, in short, and all without premeditation—simply because the only thing he ought to attend to is the preparation of a noonday lesson in formal logic which he detests."

Henry James (1843-1916)

Unlike his restless, compulsive older brother, Henry James always maintained regular working habits. He wrote every day, beginning in the morning and usually ending at about lunchtime. In his later years, severe wrist pain forced him to abandon his pen for dictation to a secretary, who would arrive each day at 9:30 A.M. After dictating all morning, James would read in the afternoon, have tea, go for a walk, eat dinner, and spend the evening making notes for the next day's work. (For a while he asked one of his secretaries to return in the evenings for further dictation; to keep her alert, he would lay bars of chocolate beside her typewriter as she worked.) Like Anthony Trollope (p. 23), James started a new book the instant the old one was finished. Asked once when he found the time to form the design of a new book, James rolled his eyes, patted the questioner on the knee, and said, "It's all *about,* it's about—it's in the air—it, so to speak, follows me and dogs me."

Franz Kafka (1883-1924)

In 1908, Kafka landed a position at the Workers' Accident Insurance Institute in Prague, where he was fortunate to be on the coveted "single shift" system, which meant office hours from 8:00 or 9:00 in the morning until 2:00 or 3:00 in the afternoon. Although this was a distinct improvement over his previous job at a different

*Franz Kafka and Felice Bauer in Budapest in
1917, near the end of their five-year, mostly
epistolary relationship*

insurance firm, which required long hours and frequent
overtime, Kafka still felt stymied; he was living with his
family in a cramped apartment, where he could muster
the concentration to write only late at night, when everyone else was asleep. As Kafka wrote to Felice Bauer in
1912, "time is short, my strength is limited, the office is a
horror, the apartment is noisy, and if a pleasant, straight-

forward life is not possible then one must try to wriggle through by subtle maneuvers." In the same letter, he goes on to describe his timetable:

> from 8 to 2 or 2:30 in the office, then lunch till 3 or 3:30, after that sleep in bed (usually only attempts; for a whole week I saw nothing but Montenegrins in my sleep, in extremely disagreeable clarity, which gave me headaches, I saw every detail of their complicated dress) till 7:30, then ten minutes of exercises, naked at the open window, then an hour's walk—alone, with Max [Brod], or with another friend, then dinner with my family (I have three sisters, one married, one engaged; the single one, without prejudicing my affection for the others, is easily my favorite); then at 10:30 (but often not till 11:30) I sit down to write, and I go on, depending on my strength, inclination, and luck, until 1, 2, or 3 o'clock, once even till 6 in the morning. Then again exercises, as above, but of course avoiding all exertions, a wash, and then, usually with a slight pain in my heart and twitching stomach muscles, to bed. Then every imaginable effort to get to sleep—i.e., to achieve the impossible, for one cannot sleep (Herr K. even demands dreamless sleep) and at the same time be thinking about one's work and trying to solve with certainty the one question that certainly is insoluble, namely, whether there will be a letter from you the next day, and at what time. Thus the night consists of two parts: one wakeful, the other sleepless, and if I were to tell you about it at length and you were prepared to listen, I should never fin-

ish. So it is hardly surprising if, at the office the next morning, I only just manage to start work with what little strength is left. In one of the corridors along which I always walk to reach my typist, there used to be a coffinlike trolley for the moving of files and documents, and each time I passed it I felt as though it had been made for me, and was waiting for me.

James Joyce (1882-1941)

"A man of small virtue, inclined to extravagance and alcoholism" is how the Irish novelist once described himself. In his daily habits, at least, he was not given to self-control or even much regularity. Left to his own devices, Joyce would typically rise late in the morning and use the afternoon (when, he said, "the mind is at its best") to write or to fulfill whatever professional obligations he might be under—often, teaching English or giving piano lessons to pay the bills. His evenings were spent socializing at cafés or restaurants, and they sometimes ended early the next morning with Joyce, who was proud of his tenor singing voice, belting out old Irish songs at the bar.

A more detailed glimpse of Joyce's routine comes from 1910, when he was living in Trieste, Italy, with his wife, Nora, their two children, and his more responsible younger brother, Stanislaus, who bailed the family out of financial straits numerous times. Joyce was struggling to find a publisher for *Dubliners,* and was teaching private piano lessons at home. The biographer Richard Ellmann describes his day:

He woke about 10 o'clock, an hour or more after Stanislaus had breakfast and left the house. Nora gave him coffee and rolls in bed, and he lay there, as Eileen [his sister] described him, "smothered in his own thoughts" until about 11 o'clock. Sometimes his Polish tailor called, and would sit discoursing on the edge of the bed while Joyce listened and nodded. About eleven he rose, shaved, and sat down at the piano (which he was buying slowly and perilously on the installment plan). As often as not his singing and playing were interrupted by the arrival of a bill collector. Joyce was notified and asked what was to be done. "Let them all come in," he would say resignedly, as if an army were at the door. The collector would come in, dun him with small success, then be skillfully steered off into a discussion of music or politics. That visit over, Joyce returned to the piano, until Nora interrupted. "Do you know there's a lesson?" or "You've put on a filthy shirt again," to which he would calmly reply, "I'll not take it off."

There was lunch at 1:00, followed by lessons from 2:00 until 7:00 or later. At the lessons, Joyce smoked long cheroots called Virginias; between pupils, he drank black coffee. About twice a week, Joyce stopped his lessons early so he and Nora could go to an opera or a play. On Sundays, he occasionally attended service at the Greek Orthodox church.

This description captures Joyce at a low ebb in his writing career. By 1914 he had begun *Ulysses,* and then he worked indefatigably on the book every day—although he still stuck to his preferred schedule of writing in the afternoons and staying out late drinking with friends. He felt he needed the nightly breaks to clear his head from literary labor that was exacting and exhausting. (Once, after two days of work yielded only two finished sentences, Joyce was asked if he had been seeking the right words. "No," he replied, "I have the words already. What I am seeking is the perfect order of words in the sentences I have.") Joyce finally finished the book in October 1921, after seven years of labor—"diversified," as he put it, "by eight illnesses and nineteen changes of address, from Austria to Switzerland, to Italy, to France." All in all, he wrote, "I calculate that I must have spent nearly 20,000 hours in writing *Ulysses*."

Marcel Proust (1871-1922)

"It is truly odious to subordinate the whole of one's life to the confection of a book," Proust wrote in 1912. It's hard to take his complaint entirely seriously. From 1908 until his death, Proust devoted the whole of his life to the writing of his monumental novel of time and memory, *Remembrance of Things Past,* eventually published in seven volumes, adding up to nearly 1.5 million words. To give his full attention to the work, Proust made a conscious decision in 1910 to withdraw from society, spending almost all his time in the famous cork-lined bedroom of his Paris apartment, sleeping during the day, working at night, and going out only when he needed to gather facts and impressions for his all-consuming work of fiction.

Upon waking in the late afternoon—typically about 3:00 or 4:00 P.M., although sometimes not until as late as 6:00—Proust first lit a batch of the opium-based Legras powders that he used to relieve his chronic asthma. Sometimes he lit just a few pinches; other times he "smoked" for hours, until the entire bedroom was thick with fumes. Then he would ring for his longtime housekeeper and confidante, Celeste, to serve the coffee. This was an elaborate ritual in its own right. Celeste would bring in a silver coffeepot holding two cups of strong black coffee; a lidded porcelain jug with a large quantity of boiled milk; and a croissant, always from the same bakery, served on its own saucer. Wordlessly, she would place these items on a bedside table and leave Proust alone to prepare his own *café au lait*. Celeste then waited in the kitchen in case Proust rang a second time, which signaled that he was ready to receive a second croissant (always kept at the ready) and a fresh jug of boiled milk to mix with the remaining coffee.

This was sometimes Proust's only sustenance for the entire day. "It isn't an exaggeration to say that he ate virtually nothing," Celeste recalled in a memoir of her life with the author. "I've never heard of anyone else living off two bowls of *café au lait* and two croissants a day. And sometimes only one croissant!" (Unbeknownst to Celeste, Proust did sometimes dine at a restaurant on the evenings he went out, and there are reports that he ate huge quantities at these occasions.) Not surprisingly, given his meager diet and sedentary habits, Proust suffered constantly from feeling cold, and he relied on an endless succession of hot water bottles and "woolies"—soft wool jumpers that he draped over his shoulders, one on top of another—to stave off the chills while he worked.

Along with the first coffee service, Celeste brought Proust his mail on a silver tray. As he dipped his croissant in his coffee, Proust would open the mail and sometimes read choice passages aloud to Celeste. Then he carefully worked his way through several daily newspapers, displaying a keen interest not only in literature and the arts but politics and finance as well. Afterward, if Proust had decided to go out that evening, he would begin the many preparations that entailed: making telephone calls, ordering the car, getting dressed. Otherwise, he began work soon after finishing with the newspaper, writing for a few hours at a stretch before ringing for Celeste to bring him something or join him for a chat. Sometimes these chats could go on for hours, particularly if Proust had recently gone out or received an interesting visitor—he seemed to use the chats as a rehearsal ground for his fiction, drawing out the nuances and hidden meaning of a conversation or encounter until he was ready to capture it on the page.

Proust wrote exclusively in bed, lying with his body almost completely horizontal and his head propped up by two pillows. To reach the exercise book resting on his lap, he had to lean awkwardly on one elbow, and his only working light was a weak, green-shaded bedside lamp. Thus any substantial period of work left his wrist cramped and his eyes exhausted. "After ten pages I am shattered," he wrote. If he felt too tired to concentrate, Proust would take a caffeine tablet, and when he was finally ready to sleep, he would counteract the caffeine with Veronal, a barbital sedative. "You're putting your foot on the brakes and the accelerator at the same time," a friend warned him. Proust didn't care—if anything, he seemed to need the work to be painful. He thought suffering had value, and that it was the root of great art. As he wrote in the final volume of *Remembrance of Things Past*, "it almost seems as though a writer's works, like the water in an artesian well, mount to a height which is in proportion to the depth to which suffering has penetrated his heart."

Samuel Beckett (1906-1989)

In 1946, Beckett began a period of intense creative activity that he would later refer to as "the siege in the room." Over the next few years he would produce his finest work—the novels *Molloy* and *Malone Dies*, and the play that would make him famous, *Waiting for Godot*. Paul Strathern describes Beckett's life during the siege:

> It was spent largely in his room, isolated from the world, coming face to face with his own demons, attempting to explore the workings of his mind. His routine was for the most part simple enough. He would rise around the early hours of the afternoon, make himself scrambled eggs, and retire to his room for as many hours as he could bear. He would then leave for his late-night perambulation of the bars of Montparnasse, drinking copious amounts of cheap red wine, returning before dawn and the long attempt to sleep. His entire life revolved around his almost psychotic obsession to write.

The siege began with an epiphany. On a late-night walk near Dublin harbor, Beckett found himself stand-

Samuel Beckett, 1950, at the end of "the siege in the room"

ing on the end of a pier in the midst of a winter storm. Amid the howling wind and churning water, he suddenly realized that the "dark he had struggled to keep under" in his life—and in his writing, which had until then failed to find an audience or meet his own aspirations—should, in fact, be the source of his creative inspiration. "I shall always be depressed," Beckett concluded, "but what comforts me is the realization that I can now accept this dark side as the commanding side of my personality. In accepting it, I will make it work for me."

Igor Stravinsky (1882-1971)

"I get up at about eight, do physical exercises, then work without a break from nine till one," Stravinsky told an interviewer in 1924. Generally, three hours of composition were the most he could manage in a day, although he would do less demanding tasks—writing letters, copying scores, practicing the piano—in the afternoon. Unless he was touring, Stravinsky worked on his compositions daily, with or without inspiration, he said. He required solitude for the task, and always closed the windows of his studio before he began: "I have never been able to compose unless sure that no one could hear me." If he felt blocked, the composer might execute a brief headstand, which, he said, "rests the head and clears the brain."

Igor Stravinsky, Los Angeles, 1966

Erik Satie (1866-1925)

In 1898, Satie moved from Paris's Montmartre district to the working-class suburb of Arcueil, where he would live for the rest of his life. Most mornings, however, the composer returned to the city on foot, walking a distance of about six miles to his former neighborhood, stopping at his favorite cafés along the way. According to one observer, Satie "walked slowly, taking small steps, his umbrella held tight under his arm. When talking he would stop, bend one knee a little, adjust his pince-nez and place his fist on his hip. Then he would take off once more, with small deliberate steps." His dress was also distinctive: the same year that he moved to Arcueil, Satie received a small inheritance, which he used to purchase a dozen identical chestnut-colored velvet suits, with the same number of matching bowler hats. Locals who saw him pass by each day soon began calling him the Velvet Gentleman.

In Paris, Satie visited friends or arranged to meet them in cafés. He would also work on his compositions in cafés, but never in restaurants—Satie was a gourmet, and he eagerly looked forward to the evening meal. (Although he appreciated fine food and was meticulous in his tastes, Satie could also apparently eat in tremendous quantities; he once consumed a thirty-egg omelet in a single sitting.) When he could, Satie earned some money in the evening playing piano for cabaret singers. Otherwise, he would make another round of the cafés, drinking a good deal. The last train back to Arcueil left at 1:00 A.M., but Satie frequently missed it. Then he would walk the several miles home, sometimes not arriving until the sun was about to rise. Nevertheless, as soon as they next morning dawned, he would set off to Paris once more.

The scholar Roger Shattuck once proposed that Satie's unique sense of musical beat, and his appreciation of "the possibility of variation within repetition," could be traced to this "endless walking back and forth across the same landscape day after day." Indeed, Satie was observed stopping to jot down ideas during his walks, pausing under a streetlamp if it was dark. During the war the streetlamps were often extinguished, and rumor had it that Satie's productivity dropped as a result.

Pablo Picasso (1881-1973)

In 1911, Picasso moved from the Bateau Lavoir, a conglomeration of low-rent studios in Paris's Montmartre district, to a much more respectable apartment on the boulevard de Clichy in Montparnasse. The new situation suited his growing fame as a painter, as well as his lifelong bourgeois aspirations. As the biographer John Richardson has written, "After the shabby gentility of his boyhood and the deprivations of his early days in Paris, Picasso wanted a lifestyle which would permit him to work in peace without material worries—'like a pauper,' he used to say, 'but with lots of money.'" The Montparnasse apartment was not without its bohemianism, however. Picasso took over its large, airy studio, forbade anyone from entering without his permission, and surrounded himself with his painting supplies, piles of miscellaneous junk, and a menagerie of pets, including a dog, three Siamese cats, and a monkey named Monina.

Throughout his life, Picasso went to bed late and got up late. At the boulevard de Clichy, he would shut himself in the studio by 2:00 P.M. and work there until at least dusk. Meanwhile, his girlfriend of seven years, Fernande, was left alone to her own devices, hanging around the apartment, waiting for Picasso to finish his work and join her for dinner. When he finally emerged from his studio, however, he was hardly good company. "He rarely spoke during meals; sometimes he would not utter a word from beginning to end," Fernande recalled. "He seemed to be bored, when he was in fact absorbed." She blamed his chronic bad mood on diet—the hypochondriacal Picasso had recently resolved to drink nothing but mineral water or milk and eat only vegetables, fish, rice pudding, and grapes.

Picasso would make more of an effort to be sociable if guests were present, as they frequently were. He had mixed feelings about entertaining. He liked to be amused between intense periods of work, but he also hated too much distraction. At Fernande's suggestion, they designated Sunday as "at-home" day (an idea borrowed from Gertrude Stein and Alice B. Toklas), "and in this way managed to dispose of the obligations of friendship in a single afternoon." Still, Richardson writes, "the artist veered between anti-social sulking and gregariousness." Painting, on the other hand, never bored or tired him. Picasso claimed that, even after three or four hours standing in front of a canvas, he did not feel the slightest fatigue.

"That's why painters live so long," he said. "While I work I leave my body outside the door, the way Moslems take off their shoes before entering the mosque."

Jean-Paul Sartre (1905-1980)

"One can be very fertile without having to work too much," Sartre once said. "Three hours in the morning, three hours in the evening. This is my only rule." If that makes the French philosopher's life sound relaxed, however, it's misleading. Sartre lived in a creative frenzy for most of his life, alternating between his daily six hours of work and an intense social life filled with rich meals, heavy drinking, drugs, and tobacco. On a typical day, Sartre worked in his Paris apartment until noon, then went out for an hour of appointments scheduled by his secretary. At 1:30, he joined his companion, Simone de Beauvoir (see p. 6), and their friends for lunch—a two-hour affair, washed down with a quart of red wine. At 3:30 on the dot he pushed away from the table and rushed back to his apartment for his second period of work, this time joined by Beauvoir. At night he slept badly, knocking himself out for a few hours with barbiturates.

By the 1950s, too much work on too little sleep—with too much wine and cigarettes—had left Sartre exhausted and on the verge of collapse. Rather than slow down, however, he turned to Corydrane, a mix of amphetamine and aspirin then fashionable among Parisian students, intellectuals, and artists (and legal in France until 1971, when it was declared toxic and taken off the market). The prescribed dose was one or two tablets in the morning and at noon. Sartre took twenty a day, beginning with his morning coffee and slowly chewing one pill after another as he worked. For each tablet, he could produce a page or two of his second major philosophical work, *The Critique of Dialectical Reason.*

This was hardly his only excess. The biographer Annie Cohen-Solal reports, "His diet over a period of twenty-four hours included two packs of cigarettes and several pipes stuffed with black tobacco, more than a quart of alcohol—wine, beer, vodka, whisky, and so on—two hundred milligrams of amphetamines, fifteen grams of aspirin, several grams of barbiturates, plus coffee, tea, rich meals." Sartre knew he was wearing himself out, but he was willing to gamble his philosophy against his health. As he said later, "I thought that in my head—not separated, not analyzed, but in a shape that would become rational—that in my head I possessed all the ideas I was to put down on paper. It was only a question of separating them and writing them on the paper. So to put it briefly, in philosophy writing consisted of analyzing my ideas; and a tube of Corydrane meant 'these ideas will be analyzed in the next two days.' "

T. S. Eliot (1888-1965)

In 1917, Eliot took a job as a clerk at Lloyds Bank, in London. During his eight years of employment there, the Missouri-born poet assumed the guise of the arche-typal English businessman: bowler hat, pin-striped suit, umbrella rolled carefully under one arm, hair parted severely on the side. Eliot took the train into the city each morning and, from the railroad station, joined the crowd crossing London Bridge (a scene he would draw on for the Unreal City portion of *The Waste Land*). "I am sojourning among the termites," he wrote to Lytton Strachey.

The literary critic I. A. Richards later recalled visiting Eliot at the bank; he found

a figure stooping, very like a dark bird in a feeder, over a big table covered with all sorts and sizes of foreign correspondence. The big table almost entirely filled a little room under the street. Within a foot of our heads when we stood were the thick, green glass squares of the pavement on which hammered all but incessantly the heels of the passers-by. There was just room for two perches beside the table.

Although Richards paints a depressing picture, Eliot was grateful for the job. Previously, he had been devoting all his energies to writing reviews and essays, teaching school, and delivering an ambitious lecture series—a devouring workload that left him little time for poetry and, worse, barely earned him enough money to scrape by. By contrast, Lloyds was a godsend. Two days after his appointment there, he wrote to his mother, "I am now earning two pounds ten shillings a week for sitting in an office from 9:15 to 5 with an hour for lunch, and tea served in the office. . . . Perhaps it will surprise you to hear that I enjoy the work. It is not nearly so fatiguing as school teaching, and is more interesting." He often used his lunch hour to discuss literary projects with friends and collaborators. In the evening he had time to work on his poetry, or to earn extra money from reviews and criticism.

It was an ideal arrangement, but over time the routine became dulling. At age thirty-four, when he had worked at the bank for five years, Eliot admitted that "the prospect of staying there for the rest of my life is abominable to me." Sensing his weariness, some of his literary friends, led by Ezra Pound, invented a scheme to free Eliot from his employment: they would create a £300 annual fund by soliciting £10 a year from thirty subscribers. When Eliot found out about the plan he was appreciative but embarrassed; he preferred the security and independence afforded by Lloyds. He remained there until 1925, when he accepted an editorial position at the publishing firm Faber and Gwyer (later Faber and Faber), where he would stay for the rest of his career.

Dmitry Shostakovich (1906–1975)

Shostakovich's contemporaries do not recall seeing him working, at least not in the traditional sense. The Russian composer was able to conceptualize a new work entirely in his head, and then write it down with extreme rapidity—if uninterrupted, he could average twenty or thirty pages of score a day, making virtually no corrections as he went. "I always found it amazing that he never needed to try things out on the piano," his younger sister recalled. "He just sat down, wrote out whatever he heard in his head, and then played it through complete on the piano." But this feat was apparently preceded by hours or days of mental composition—during which he "appeared to be a man of great inner tensions," the musicologist Alexei Ikonnikov observed, "with his continually moving, 'speaking' hands, which were never at rest."

Mikhail Meyerovich, a fellow composer, had much the same impression. He spent time with Shostakovich in 1945 at an artists' retreat. "I discovered him to be a very lively man who was always in motion and could not spend a minute without some occupation," Meyerovich wrote. It was a mystery how he managed to compose so much music. Intrigued, Meyerovich began to watch him closely:

> He would play football and fool around with friends; then he would suddenly disappear. After forty minutes or so he would turn up again. "How are you

Dmitry Shostakovich, circa 1930s

doing? Let me kick the ball." Then we would have dinner and drink some wine and take a walk, and he would be the life and soul of the party. Every now and then he would disappear for a while and then join us again. Towards the end of my stay, he disappeared altogether. We didn't see him for a week. Then he turned up, unshaven and looking exhausted.

Shostakovich had just completed his Second Quartet. Although his fellow composers were amazed by the speed and sureness with which he conceived new works, Shostakovich himself was afraid that perhaps he worked too fast. "I worry about the lightning speed with which I compose," he confessed in a letter to a friend.

> Undoubtedly this is bad. One shouldn't compose as quickly as I do. Composition is a serious process, and in the words of a ballerina friend of mine, "You can't keep going at a gallop." I compose with diabolical speed and can't stop myself. . . . It is exhausting, rather unpleasant, and at the end of the day you lack any confidence in the result. But I can't rid myself of the bad habit.

Henry Green (1905-1973)

Green led a double life. As Henry Yorke—his birth name—he was a wealthy aristocrat who spent his days at the offices of his family's manufacturing business. (Called Pontifex, its chief product was a high-pressure filling machine for beer bottling.) As Henry Green, however, he wrote nine utterly original novels, including *Loving, Living,* and *Party Going.* Given his inherited income, one may wonder why Green bothered going in to the office at all—he certainly didn't need the money. Jeremy Treglown offers an answer in his 2000 biography:

> Though he occasionally spoke to his friends about giving up Pontifex and living off his unearned income in order to do nothing but write, he was beginning to find that the office routines of Henry Yorke were useful, even essential, to the imaginative work of Henry Green. He feared his own volatility and often referred to his need for habitual routines to keep him sane. The job gave him day-to-day stability as well as experiences that he could use in his writing. It was also much less demanding than fiction. He told Mary Strickland that writing entries for engineering catalogs was "the greatest fun."

Green's reliance on the stability of a day job was no doubt helped by the fact that his actual duties were practically zero. According to Treglown, a typical day in the life of Henry Yorke, managing director of Pontifex, looked something like this: He arrived at work at about 10:00 A.M., was brought his gin, and spent an hour or two pottering about his office or gossiping with the secretaries. At 11:30, he left to spend the middle part of the workday at a nearby pub, refreshing himself with a couple of pints of beer before returning to gin. A colleague or two would eventually join him there, and they would talk about people at work or the bar regulars, whose conversation Green would have been eavesdropping on while he was alone. When the managing director finally returned to the office, he repeated his morning routine and then—maybe—wrote a page or two of his novel before catching the bus home.

The remainder of Green's writing occurred at night. After dinner and any social engagements, he would settle into his armchair with a notebook and a cheap pen wrapped with a bandage (to make it easier to grip) and scribble away until about midnight. When asked, years later, why he had chosen to publish under a pseudonym, Green said that he didn't want his business associates to know about his novel writing. They eventually found out anyway, much to Green's distress. An interviewer later asked if this discovery affected his business relationships:

> Yes, yes, oh yes—why, some years ago a group at our Birmingham works put in a penny each and bought a copy of a book of mine, *Living*. And as I was going round the iron foundry one day, a loam molder said to me, "I read your book, Henry." "And did you like it?" I asked, rightly apprehensive. He replied, "I didn't think much of it, Henry." Too awful.

Agatha Christie (1890–1976)

In her autobiography, Christie admitted that even after she had written ten books, she didn't really consider herself a "bona fide author." When filling out forms that asked for her occupation, it never occurred to her to put down anything other than "married woman." "The funny thing is that I have little memory of the books I wrote just after my marriage," she added. "I suppose I was enjoying myself so much in ordinary living that writing was a task which I performed in spells and bursts. I never had a definite place which was *my* room or where I retired specially to write."

This caused her endless trouble with journalists, who inevitably wanted to photograph the author at her desk. But there was no such place. "All I needed was a steady table and a typewriter," she wrote. "A marble-topped bedroom washstand table made a good place to write; the dining-room table between meals was also suitable."

Many friends have said to me, "I never know when you write your books, because I've never seen you writing, or even seen you go away to write." I must behave rather as dogs do when they retire with a bone; they depart in a secretive manner and you do not see them again for an odd half hour. They return self-consciously with mud on their noses. I do much the same. I felt slightly embarrassed if I was going to write. Once I could get away, however, shut the door and get people not to interrupt me, then I was able to go full speed ahead, completely lost in what I was doing.

Somerset Maugham (1874-1965)

"Maugham thought that writing, like drinking, was an easy habit to form and a difficult one to break," Jeffrey Meyers noted in his 2004 biography of the British writer. "It was more an addiction than a vocation." The addiction served him well; in his nearly ninety-two years, Maugham published seventy-eight books. He wrote for three or four hours every morning, setting himself a daily requirement of one thousand to one thousand five hundred words. He would get a start on the day's work before he even sat down at his desk, thinking of the first two sentences he wanted to write while soaking in the bath. Then, once at work, there was little to distract him—Maugham believed that it was impossible to write while looking at a view, so his desk always faced a blank wall. When he wrapped up his morning's work at about noon, Maugham often felt impatient to begin again. "When you're writing, when you're creating a character, it's with you constantly, you're preoccupied with it, it's alive," he said—adding that when you "cut that out of your life, it's a rather lonely life."

Graham Greene (1904-1991)

In 1939, with World War II fast approaching, Greene began to worry that he would die before he could complete what he was certain would be his greatest novel, *The Power and the Glory,* and that his wife and children would be left in poverty. So he set out to write another of his "entertainments"—melodramatic thrillers that lacked artistry but that he knew would make money—while continuing to grind away at his masterpiece. To escape the distractions of home life, Greene rented a private studio whose address and telephone number he kept secret from everyone but his wife. There he maintained regular office hours, devoting his mornings to the thriller *The Confidential Agent* and his afternoons to *The Power and the Glory*. To manage the pressure of writing two books at once, he took Benzedrine tablets twice daily, one upon waking and the other at midday. As a result he was able to write two thousand words in the morning alone, as opposed to his usual five hundred. After only six weeks, *The Confidential Agent* was completed and on its way to being published. (*The Power and the Glory* took another four months.)

Greene did not keep up this kind of productivity (or the drug use) throughout his career. By his sixties he admitted that, where he once required five hundred words of himself each day, he was now setting the bar as low as two hundred words. In 1968, an interviewer asked if he was "a nine-till-five man." "No," Greene replied. "Good heavens, I would say I was a nine-till-a-quarter-past-ten man."

Joseph Cornell (1903-1972)

Cornell made his first shadow box in 1934, not long after securing a nine-to-five job in the home-furnishings division of a Manhattan textile studio. It was tedious and

Joseph Cornell's basement workroom in Queens, 1969.
Photograph by Hans Namuth.

low-paying work, but Cornell stayed there for six years. He felt obligated to be the wage earner for his household—he lived with his mother and handicapped brother in a small house in Flushing, Queens—and he was still a relative unknown in the art world.

That would change over the next several years as Cornell worked nights at the kitchen table, sorting and assembling materials for his boxes. It was not easy going. Some nights he felt too fatigued from his day job to concentrate on his art and would sit up reading instead, switching on the oven for warmth. In the mornings, his quarrelsome mother would scold him about the mess he'd left at the kitchen table; without a proper workroom, Cornell was forced to store his growing collection of magazine clippings and dime-store baubles out in the garage.

It wasn't until 1940 that Cornell finally mustered the courage to quit his job and pursue his art full-time—and even then his habits changed little. He still worked nights at the kitchen table, while his mother and brother slept upstairs. In the late morning he would head downtown for breakfast at his local Bickford's restaurant, often satisfying his sweet tooth with a Danish or a slice of pie (and lovingly cataloging these indulgences in his diary). Afternoons were spent on the freelance commercial work that paid the bills and helped Cornell justify his lack of a day job to his mother. Still, as much as he had hated working, Cornell found that he hated not working too. During the 1940s, he returned to the workforce twice, happy at first to resume the reassuring nine-to-five routine. Then, after a period of months, he would grow frustrated and quit. Eventually he reconciled himself to the solitary artist's life. The addition of a basement workroom made it possible for Cornell to work on his boxes during the day, and his frequent and wide-ranging correspondence—not to mention the steady stream of artists, curators, and collectors that began making the pilgrimage out to Flushing—kept him connected to the world outside his mother's house.

Sylvia Plath (1932-1963)

Plath's journal, which she kept from age eleven until her suicide at age thirty, records a near-constant struggle to find and stick to a productive writing schedule. "From now on: see if this is possible: set alarm for 7:30 and get up then, tired or not," she wrote in one example, from January 1959. "Rip through breakfast and housecleaning (bed and dishes, mopping or whatever) by 8:30. . . . Be writing before 9 (nine), that takes the curse off it." But the curse was never off it for long, despite Plath's frequent attempts to carve out a chunk of inviolable writing time each day. Only near the end of her life, living separated from her husband, the poet Ted Hughes, and taking care of their two small children alone, did Plath find a routine that worked for her. She was using sedatives to get to sleep, and when they wore off at about 5:00 A.M. she would get up and write until the children awoke. Working like this for two months in the autumn of 1962, she produced nearly all the poems of *Ariel,* the posthumously published collection that finally established her as a major and searingly original new voice in poetry. For once Plath felt possessed by her work, triumphant in the creative act. She wrote to her mother in October 1962, four months before she would take her own life, "I am a genius of a writer; I have it in me. I am writing the best poems of my life; they will make my name."

John Cheever (1912-1982)

"When I was younger," Cheever recalled in 1978, "I used to wake up at eight, work until noon, and then break, hollering with pleasure; then I'd go back to work through to five, get pissed, get laid, go to bed, and do the same thing again the next day." In the summer of 1945, when he moved with his wife and young daughter to a ninth-floor apartment on Manhattan's East Side, the thirty-three-year-old Cheever adopted a somewhat more businesslike routine. As Blake Bailey writes in his 2009 biography, "Almost every morning for the next five years, he'd put on his only suit and ride the elevator with other men leaving for work; Cheever, however, would proceed all the way down to a storage room in the basement, where he'd doff his suit and write in his boxers until noon, then dress again and ascend for lunch." After that he had the rest of the day free, and he would often take his young daughter on long walks around the city, bringing her along to the Menemsha Bar on 57th Street if he felt like a drink on the way home.

Cheever continued to write pretty much every morning for the rest of his life—but as his career progressed, the writing sessions grew shorter and shorter, while cocktail hour began earlier and earlier. By the 1960s, Cheever's working day was usually over by 10:30 A.M., after which he would lurk about the house (the family had since moved to the suburbs), pretending to read while waiting for an opportunity to slip unnoticed into the pantry and pour himself a few "scoops" of gin. His journals, begun in the late 1940s and continued for the ensuing three decades, record his constant struggle with alcoholism and his attempts to "achieve some equilibrium between writing and living." The following entry, from 1971, describes a typical day:

> The hour between five and six is my best. It is dark. A few birds sing. I feel contented and loving. My discontents begin at seven, when light fills the room. I am unready for the day—unready to face it soberly, that is. Some days I would like to streak down to the pantry and pour a drink. I recite the incantations I recorded three years ago, and it was three years ago that I described the man who thought continuously of bottles. The situation is, among other things, repetitious. The hours between seven and ten, when I begin to drink, are the worst. I could take a Miltown [a tranquilizer], but I do not. . . . I would like to pray, but to whom—some God of the Sunday school classroom, some provincial king whose prerogatives and rites remain unclear? I am afraid of cars, planes, boats, snakes, stray dogs, falling leaves, extension ladders, and the sound of the wind in the chimney; Dr. Gespaden, I am afraid of the wind in the chimney. I sleep off my hooch after lunch and very often awake feeling content once more, and loving, although I do not work. Swimming is the apex of the day, its heart, and after this—night is falling—I am stoned but serene. So I sleep and dream until five.

The journals also chart Cheever's anxiety about his complicated sexuality. Cheever stayed married for more than forty years, and he slept with other women, but he also struggled with homosexual longings and had several affairs with men. To make matters worse, he had what appears to have been an unusually robust sex drive (the actress Hope Lange, who had a brief affair with Cheever, said that he was "the horniest man [she] ever met") combined with frequent bouts of impotence, probably brought on by his alcoholism but no doubt made worse by his sexual guilt and a frequently rocky marriage. All of this was distracting from his work, especially since Cheever placed a high value on the salutary effects of erotic release. He thought that his constitution required at least "two or three orgasms a week" and he believed that sexual stimulation improved his concentration and even his eyesight: "With a stiff prick I can read the small print in prayer books but with a limp prick I can barely read newspaper headlines."

Cheever occasionally grew weary of his oversize appetites, but he also seemed to think that his inner turmoil was somehow tied to his imaginative faculties—that he possessed a wellspring of innate vitality that fed his fiction but also overflowed into recklessness and addiction. Sometimes he couldn't decide if the writing was a valuable outlet for his energies or if indulging his imagination in fiction actually made things worse. "I must convince myself that writing is not, for a man of my disposition, a self-destructive vocation," he wrote in his journal in 1968. "I hope and think it is not, but I am not genuinely sure."

Louis Armstrong (1901-1971)

The greater part of Armstrong's adult life was spent on the road, traveling from one gig to another, sleeping in a succession of anonymous hotel rooms. To manage the stress and boredom of this lifestyle, Armstrong evolved an elaborate pre- and post-show ritual, described by Terry Teachout in his 2009 biography. He took pains to arrive at any engagement two hours before starting time, already bathed and dressed, so that he could hole up in his dressing room, dosing himself with the home remedies he always swore by: swigs of glycerin and honey to "wash out the pipes," Maalox for occasional stomach pains, and, for his chronic lip problems, a special salve made by a trombone player in Germany. When the show was over, he returned to the dressing room to greet friends and fans, sitting in his undershirt with a handkerchief tied on his head, fiddling with his trumpet. Armstrong never ate dinner before a show, but he would sometimes go out for a late supper afterward or, more often, retreat to his hotel room for a room-service meal or take-out Chinese food, his second-favorite cuisine (after red beans and rice). Then he would roll a joint—Armstrong openly smoked pot, or "gage," as he called it, nearly every day, believing it to be far superior to alcohol—catch up on his voluminous correspondence, and listen to music on the two reel-to-reel tape recorders that followed him wherever he went.

A lifelong insomniac, Armstrong relied on music to lull himself to sleep. Before he could get into bed, however, he had to administer the last of his daily home remedies, Swiss Kriss, a potent herbal laxative invented by the nutritionist Gayelord Hauser in 1922 (and still on the market today). Armstrong believed so strongly in its curative powers that he recommended it to all his friends, and even had a card printed up with a photo of himself sitting on the toilet, above the caption "Leave It All Behind Ya." His doctors were horrified by his daily self-medication, but the routine seemed to work for him; night after night, he continued to perform at a remarkably high level despite the wearying tour schedule. As he told an interviewer in 1969, "It's been hard goddam work, man. Feel like I spent 20,000 years on planes and railroads, like I blowed my chops off. . . . I never tried to prove nothing, just always wanted to give a good show. My life has been my music, it's always come first, but the music ain't worth nothing if you can't lay it on the public."

W. B. Yeats (1865-1939)

In 1912, Yeats described his routine in a letter to his fellow poet Edwin Ellis: "I read from 10 to 11. I write from 11 till 2, then after lunch I read till 3:30. Then I go into the woods or fish in the lake till 5. Then I write letters or work a little till 7 when I go out for an hour before dinner." According to another literary friend, Yeats always made sure to write for at least two hours every day, whether he felt inclined to it or not. This daily discipline was crucial for Yeats both because his concentration faltered without a regular schedule—"Every change upsets my never very resolute habits of work"—and because he worked at a snail's pace. "I am a very slow writer," he noted in 1899.

"I have never done more than five or six good lines in a day." This meant that a lyric poem of eighty or more lines took about three months of hard labor. Fortunately, Yeats was not so careful about his other writing, like the literary criticism he did to earn extra money. "One has to give something of one's self to the devil that one may live," he said. "I give my criticism."

Wallace Stevens (1879-1955)

In 1916, when he was thirty-six years old, Stevens accepted a position at the Hartford Accident and Indemnity Company, where he remained employed as an insurance lawyer until his death. Far from stifling his creativity, the job seemed to suit Stevens's temperament and even encourage his poetry. "I find that having a job is one of the best things in the world that could happen to me," he once said. "It introduces discipline and regularity into one's life. I am just as free as I want to be and of course I have nothing to worry about about money."

Stevens was an early riser—he woke at 6:00 every morning to read for two hours—and unfailingly punctual in his work habits. He arrived at the office at 9:00 A.M. sharp and left at 4:30. Between work and home he walked, a distance of three or four miles each way. Most days, he took an additional hour-long walk on his lunch break. It was on these walks that he composed his poetry, stopping now and then to scribble lines on one of the half-dozen or so envelopes he always had stuffed in his pocket. At work, too, he would occasionally pause to write down fragments of poems, which he kept filed in the lower right-hand drawer of his desk, and he would routinely hand his secretary these various scraps of verse for typing. Although his colleagues were aware of his poetry, Stevens assiduously avoided talking about it, preferring to maintain the face of a mild-mannered, somewhat aloof businessman in all his public dealings with the world.

Kingsley Amis (1922-1995)

"Do you have a daily routine?" an interviewer asked Amis in 1975.

> Yes. I don't get up very early. I linger over breakfast reading the papers, telling myself hypocritically that I've got to keep up with what's going on, but really staving off the dreadful time when I have to go to the typewriter. That's probably about ten-thirty, still in pajamas and dressing gown. And the agreement I have with myself is that I can stop whenever I like and go and shave and so on. In practice, it's not till about one or one-fifteen that I do that—I usually try and time it with some music on the radio. Then I emerge, and nicotine and alcohol are produced. I work on until about two or two-fifteen, have lunch, then if there's urgency about, I have to write in the afternoon, which I really hate doing—I really dislike afternoons, whatever's happening. But then the agreement is that it doesn't matter how little gets done in the afternoon. And later on, with luck, a

cup of tea turns up, and then it's only a question of drinking more cups of tea until the bar opens at six o'clock and one can get into second gear. I go on until about eight-thirty and I always hate stopping. It's not a question of being carried away by one's creative afflatus, but saying, "Oh dear, next time I do this I shall be feeling tense again."

As he reached his seventies, Amis's routine shifted somewhat, with the drinking taking a more prominent role even as he continued to write daily. He would rise a little before 8:00, shower and shave, eat breakfast (grapefruit, cereal, banana, tea), read the newspaper, and sit down in his study by about 9:30. Picking up where he left off the previous evening—he always made sure to stop writing when he knew what would come next, making it easier to begin the next day—Amis would work at his typewriter for a few hours, shooting for his minimum daily requirement of five hundred words, which he usually managed by 12:30. Then a taxi would take him to the pub or to the all-male Garrick Club, where he would have his first drink of the day (a Macallan malt with a splash of water). He might have one drink before lunch, or he might have two or three. Then there was wine with lunch, followed by coffee, and, perhaps, a glass or two of claret or burgundy. All this over—it's now somewhere between 3:15 and 3:45—Amis took a taxi back home for a thirty-minute nap in his favorite armchair. Then he returned to his study for a final stint at the typewriter, beginning at 5:00 and lasting for an hour or two. With his writing day now over, Amis poured himself another Scotch-and-water and settled down to watch his favorite television programs before dinner with the family, followed by more television or perhaps a video. Amis's final Scotch-and-water came at about 11:00; it would last him until half-past midnight, when some sleeping pills would finally put him out. If he woke in the middle of the night with a full bladder, he needn't travel all the way to the bathroom; he kept a bucket by the bed for just these occasions.

Martin Amis (b. 1949)

Unlike his father, Martin Amis does not approach his writing with a feeling of dread: "I seldom have that kind of squeamishness," he told *The Paris Review* in 1998. Amis said that he writes every weekday, driving himself to an office less than a mile from his London apartment. He keeps business hours but generally writes for only a small portion of that time. "Everyone assumes I'm a systematic and nose-to-the-grindstone kind of person," he said. "But to me it seems like a part-time job, really, in that writing from eleven to one continuously is a very good day's work. Then you can read or play tennis or snooker. Two hours. I think most writers would be very happy with two hours of concentrated work."

Umberto Eco (b. 1932)

The Italian philosopher and novelist—who is perhaps best known for his first novel, *The Name of the Rose*, published when he was forty-eight years old—claims that he follows no set writing routine. "There is no rule," he said in 2008. "For me it would be impossible to have a schedule. It can happen that I start writing at seven o'clock in the morning and I finish at three o'clock at night, stopping only to eat a sandwich. Sometimes I don't feel the need to write at all." When pressed by the interviewer, however, Eco admitted that his writing habits are not always so variable.

> If I am in my countryside home, at the top of the hills of Montefeltro, then I have a certain routine. I turn on my computer, I look at my e-mails, I start reading something, and then I write until the afternoon. Later I go to the village, where I have a glass at the bar and read the newspaper. I come back home and I watch TV or a DVD in the evening until eleven, and then I work a little more until one or two o'clock in the morning. There I have a certain routine because I am not interrupted. When I am in Milan or at the university, I am not master of my own time—there is always somebody else deciding what I should do.

Even without blocks of free time, however, Eco says that he is able to be productive during the brief "interstices" in the day. He told *The Paris Review*'s interviewer: "This morning you rang, but then you had to wait for the elevator, and several seconds elapsed before you showed up at the door. During those seconds, waiting for you, I was thinking of this new piece I'm writing. I can work in the water closet, in the train. While swimming I produce a lot of things, especially in the sea. Less so in the bathtub, but there too."

Woody Allen (b. 1935)

When he's not shooting a film, most of Allen's creative energy goes toward mentally working out the problems of a new story. This is the hard part; once he's satisfied with the story elements, the writing itself comes easy (and the filmmaking is mostly a chore). But to get the story right requires "obsessive thinking," Allen has said. To keep from getting stuck in a rut, he's developed a few reliable tricks.

I've found over the years that any momentary change stimulates a fresh burst of mental energy. So if I'm in this room and then I go into the other room, it helps me. If I go outside to the street, it's a huge help. If I go up and take a shower it's a big help. So I sometimes take extra showers. I'll be down here [in the living room] and at an impasse and what will help me is to go upstairs and take a shower. It breaks up everything and relaxes me.

The shower is particularly good in cold weather. This sounds so silly, but I'll be working dressed as I am and I'll want to get into the shower for a creative stint. So I'll take off some of my clothes and make myself an English muffin or something and try to give myself a little chill so I want to get in the shower. I'll stand there with steaming hot water coming down for thirty minutes, forty-five minutes, just thinking out ideas and working on plot. Then I get out and dry myself and dress and then flop down on the bed and think there.

Going out for a walk works just as well, although Allen can no longer walk the streets without being recognized and approached, which ruins his concentration. He'll often pace the terrace of his apartment as a substitute. And he uses any little free moments in the day to return to the story he's working on. "I think in the cracks all the time," he has said. "I never stop."

David Lynch (b. 1946)

"I like things to be orderly," Lynch told a reporter in 1990.

> For seven years I ate at Bob's Big Boy. I would go at 2:30, after the lunch rush. I ate a chocolate shake and four, five, six, seven cups of coffee—with lots of sugar. And there's lots of sugar in that chocolate shake. It's a thick shake. In a silver goblet. I would get a rush from all this sugar, and I would get so many ideas! I would write them on these napkins. It was like I had a desk with paper. All I had to do was remember to bring my pen, but a waitress would give me one if I remembered to return it at the end of my stay. I got a lot of ideas at Bob's.

Lynch's other means of getting ideas is Transcendental Meditation, which he has practiced daily since 1973. "I have never missed a meditation in thirty-three years," he wrote in his 2006 book, *Catching the Big Fish*. "I meditate once in the morning and again in the afternoon, for about twenty minutes each time. Then I go about the business of my day." If he's shooting a film, he will sometimes sneak in a third session at the end of the day. "We waste so much time on other things, anyway," he writes. "Once you add this and have a routine, it fits in very naturally."

Maya Angelou (b. 1928)

Angelou has never been able to write at home. "I try to keep home very pretty," she has said, "and I can't work in a pretty surrounding. It throws me." As a result, she has always worked in hotel or motel rooms, the more anonymous the better. She described her routine in a 1983 interview:

> I usually get up at about 5:30, and I'm ready to have coffee by 6, usually with my husband. He goes off to his work around 6:30, and I go off to mine. I keep a hotel room in which I do my work—a tiny, mean room with just a bed, and sometimes, if I can find it, a face basin. I keep a dictionary, a Bible, a deck of cards and a bottle of sherry in the room. I try to get there around 7, and I work until 2 in the afternoon. If the work is going badly, I stay until 12:30. If it's going well, I'll stay as long as it's going well. It's lonely, and it's marvelous. I edit while I'm working. When I come home at 2, I read over what I've written that day, and then try to put it out of my mind. I shower, prepare dinner, so that when my husband comes home, I'm not totally absorbed

Maya Angelou at work, 1974

in my work. We have a semblance of a normal life. We have a drink together and have dinner. Maybe after dinner I'll read to him what I've written that day. He doesn't comment. I don't invite comments from anyone but my editor, but hearing it aloud is good. Sometimes I hear the dissonance; then I try to straighten it out in the morning.

In this manner, Angelou has managed to write not only her acclaimed series of autobiographies but numerous poems, plays, lectures, articles, and television scripts. Sometimes the intensity of the work brings on strange physical reactions—her back goes out, her knees swell, and her eyelids once swelled completely shut. Still, she enjoys pushing herself to the limits of her ability. "I have always got to be the best," she has said. "I'm absolutely compulsive, I admit it. I don't see that's a negative."

George Balanchine (1904-1983)

Balanchine liked to do his own laundry. "When I'm ironing, that's when I do most of my work," he once said. The choreographer rose early, before 6:00 A.M., made a pot of tea, and read a little or played a hand of Russian solitaire while he gathered his thoughts. Then he did his ironing for the day (he did his own washing too, in a portable machine in his Manhattan apartment) and, between 7:30 and 8:00, phoned his longtime assistant for a rundown of the day's schedule. Most weekdays he would make the five-minute walk from his apartment to Lincoln Center, where he kept an office in the State Theater. He often taught a class there at 11:00, then spent the better part of the afternoon in the rehearsal studio, choreographing his latest ballet. The work went slowly; two hours of rehearsal might amount to only two minutes of actual ballet on stage. But Balanchine never lacked for inspiration. "My muse must come to me on union time," he said.

Al Hirschfeld (1903-2003)

The great American caricaturist—who immortalized virtually all of the major Broadway and Hollywood stars of his era—continued to work right up to his death, at age ninety-nine, driving himself from his uptown Manhattan brownstone to the theater district most nights (and finding a parking spot on the street), using a system of personal shorthand to create preliminary sketches in the dark, and turning those sketches into finished drawings in his studio the next day. In 1999, Mel Gussow described Hirschfeld's habits as a nonagenarian artist:

> In his 90s, he continues his daily routine, working a full day in his studio, breaking only for lunch

Al Hirschfeld at home, New York City, 1998

and having tea at his worktable (with a supply of caramels for snacks). Except for the telephone, he remains isolated and seldom breaks his regimen to go out to eat or to a museum. Evenings are reserved for theatergoing and socializing. When he is not at the theater, he is usually having dinner at home with friends. After the theater, if he does not go to an opening night party, he is home in time to watch the news and *Nightline* on television. Then he reads from midnight to two, favoring philosophical works, often rereading Thoreau or Bertrand Russell.

According to his second wife, Hirschfeld even worked on his drawings in his sleep. "Very often, when an assignment is difficult, he can't fall asleep until the artistic problem is solved, or he *dreams* about various ways of designing his drawing," she wrote in 1999. "Now that's what I call a hard worker! Even his subconscious doesn't give him any time off. The next morning, holding onto that dream, he rises at first light and races to his drawing board to jot down all those nocturnal notions. In his youth, he was called 'the flash,' which still describes not only his working habits, but how quickly he finds a parking space."

Truman Capote (1924-1984)

"I am a completely horizontal author," Capote told *The Paris Review* in 1957. "I can't think unless I'm lying down, either in bed or stretched out on a couch and with a cigarette and coffee handy. I've got to be puffing and sipping. As the afternoon wears on, I shift from coffee to mint tea to sherry to martinis." Capote typically wrote for four hours during the day, then revised his work in the evenings or the next morning, eventually doing two longhand versions in pencil before typing up a final copy. (Even the typing was done in bed, with the typewriter balanced on his knees.)

Writing in bed was the least of Capote's superstitions. He couldn't allow three cigarette butts in the same ashtray at once, and if he was a guest at someone's house, he would stuff the butts in his pocket rather than overfill the tray. He couldn't begin or end anything on a Friday. And he compulsively added numbers in his head, refusing to dial a telephone number or accept a hotel room if the digits made a sum he considered unlucky. "It's endless, the things I can't and won't," he said. "But I derive some curious comfort from obeying these primitive concepts."

Richard Wright (1908-1960)

Wright wrote the first draft of *Native Son* in 1938, completing 576 pages in a mere five months. Thanks to a program of the New York Writers' Project, he was getting paid to work on his fiction full-time; he had only to sign in at the Project's Midtown office once a week to continue collecting his stipend.

At the time, he was living in the Brooklyn apartment of the Newton family, whom he had befriended years earlier in Chicago. Herbert Newton was a prominent black

Communist busy with Party duties; he left the house at about 9:00 A.M. and did not come home until late. His wife, Jane, stayed home with their three children. As Hazel Rowley details in her 2001 biography, Wright got up by 6:00 A.M. and promptly left the house, to avoid the domestic chaos that erupted when the Newton children woke. Carrying his writing supplies—a yellow legal pad, a fountain pen, and a bottle of ink—Wright walked to nearby Fort Greene Park, where he would install himself on a bench at the top of the hill and write for four hours.

He stuck to this routine in all weather, returning to the apartment at 10:00 A.M.—on rainy days, dripping wet from sitting outside—for breakfast and to read his morning's work to Jane Newton. With the kids clamoring about them, they would discuss new developments in the plot, sometimes arguing about the direction Wright wanted to take the book. Then Wright would head upstairs to his bedroom to type what he had written in the morning. Afterward he visited the public library or saw friends, sometimes returning to the apartment for a 5:00 P.M. supper with Jane and the children. When, after six months, the family moved to a new apartment, Wright went with them, holing up in a back bedroom to revise his manuscript, working as many as fifteen hours a day. "I never intend to work that long and hard again," he wrote to a friend.

H. L. Mencken (1880-1956)

Mencken's routine was simple: work for twelve or four-teen hours a day, every day, and in the late evening, enjoy a drink and conversation. This was his lifestyle as a young bachelor—when he belonged to a drinking club and often met his fellow members at a saloon after work—and it hardly changed when he got married, at age fifty, to a fellow writer. Then the couple worked for three or four hours in the morning, ate lunch, took naps, worked for another few hours, ate dinner, and returned to work until 10:00, when they would meet in the drawing room to talk and have a drink.

Mencken typically divided his working day as follows: reading manuscripts and answering mail in the morning (he replied to every letter he received on the same day, fir-ing off at least one hundred thousand missives in his life), editorial chores in the afternoon, and concentrated writ-ing in the evening. Unbelievably, he claimed to have a lazy temperament. "Like most men, I am lazy by nature and seize every opportunity to loaf," he wrote in a 1932 letter. But this only made him work harder; believing that he was inclined to indolence, Mencken didn't allow himself the luxury of free time. His compulsiveness meant that he was astonishingly productive throughout his life—and yet, at age sixty-four, he could nevertheless write, "Look-ing back over a life of hard work . . . my only regret is that I didn't work even harder."

Philip Larkin (1922-1985)

"I work all day, and get half drunk at night," Larkin wrote in his 1977 poem "Aubade." A few years later he described his real-life (and not so dissimilar) routine to *The Paris Review*:

> My life is as simple as I can make it. Work all day, cook, eat, wash up, telephone, hack writing, drink, television in the evenings. I almost never go out. I suppose everyone tries to ignore the passing of time—some people by doing a lot, being in California one year and Japan the next. Or there's my way—making every day and every year exactly the same. Probably neither works.

Larkin worked as a librarian for almost his entire adult life, realizing early on that he would never be able to make a living from his writing alone. "I was brought up to think you had to have a job, and write in your spare time, like Trollope," he said. Although he admitted to wondering what would have happened had he been able to write full-time, he also thought that two hours of composition in the evenings, after dinner and the dishes, was plenty: "After that you're going round in circles, and it's much better to leave it for twenty-four hours, by which time your subconscious or whatever has solved the block and you're ready to go on."

Frank Lloyd Wright (1867–1959)

A friend of Wright's once observed that as long as she had known him, the architect seemed to spend the entire day doing everything but actually working on his building designs. He held meetings, took phone calls, answered letters, supervised students—but was rarely seen at the drafting table. The friend wanted to know: When did Wright conceive the ideas and make the sketches for his buildings? "Between 4 and 7 o'clock in the morning," he told her. "I go to sleep promptly when I go to bed. Then I wake up around 4 and can't sleep. But my mind's clear, so I get up and work for three or four hours. Then I go to bed for another nap." During the afternoon he would often take an additional nap, lying down on a thinly padded wooden bench or even a concrete ledge; the uncomfortable perch, he said, prevented him from oversleeping.

Another reason that Wright was rarely seen working on his designs is that the architect never made so much as a sketch until he had the entire project worked out in his head. Numerous colleagues have reported, with some consternation, his habit of postponing project drawings until right before a crucial client meeting. (For Fallingwater, perhaps the most famous residence of the twentieth century, Wright didn't begin the drawings until the client called to say he was getting in the car and would be arriving for their meeting in a little more than two hours.) Wright did not get frazzled by these forced bursts of last-minute productivity; indeed, colleagues and family reported that he never seemed hurried, and that he seemed to have an almost inexhaustible supply of creative energy.

Apparently, Wright's energies were equally prodigious in the bedroom—so much so that the architect's third wife eventually began to worry about him. Even at age eighty-five, she claimed, Wright could still make love to her two or three times a day. "Perhaps it was a dispensation from heaven," she wrote. "But his passionate desire became so potent that I even got worried that such a tremendous outpouring of sex energy might be harmful to him." She sought the advice of a doctor, who suggested giving Wright a dose of "saltpeter," or potassium nitrate, which was thought to reduce a man's sex drive. In the end, she couldn't bring herself to do it: "I could not think of myself dulling or in any way depriving him of that great experience."

Louis I. Kahn (1901-1974)

Like a lot of architects, Kahn worked as a university professor at the same time that he maintained a busy private practice. During his professorship at the University of Pennsylvania, Kahn would teach during the day, head home in the afternoon, then go into his office at night and begin a new "day" of work at 10:30 P.M. When he got tired, he would sleep on a bench in his office for a few hours before moving back to the drafting table. This was both inspiring and intimidating for his employees, who were expected to put in similarly long hours. One of Kahn's associates remembered, "Lou had so much energy that it was hard for him to see that other people might not have as much."

George Gershwin (1898-1937)

"To me George was a little sad all the time because he had this compulsion to work," Ira Gershwin said of his brother. "He never relaxed." Indeed, Gershwin typically worked for twelve hours or more a day, beginning in the late morning and going until past midnight. He started the day with a breakfast of eggs, toast, coffee, and orange juice, then immediately began composing, sitting at the piano in his pajamas, bathrobe, and slippers. He would take breaks for a mid-afternoon lunch, a late-afternoon walk, and supper at about 8:00. If Gershwin had a party to attend in the evening, it was not unusual for him to return home after midnight and plunge back into work until dawn. He was dismissive of inspiration, saying that if he waited for the muse he would compose at most three songs a year. It was better to work every day. "Like the pugilist," Gershwin said, "the songwriter must always keep in training."

Joseph Heller (1923-1999)

Heller wrote *Catch*-22 in the evenings after work, sitting at the kitchen table in his Manhattan apartment. "I spent two or three hours a night on it for eight years," he said. "I gave up once and started watching television with my wife. Television drove me back to *Catch*-22. I couldn't imagine what Americans did at night when they weren't writing novels." During the day he worked in the advertising departments of *Time, Look,* and, finally, *McCall's.* Although *Catch-22* skewers bureaucracies similar to the ones he worked for, Heller was not miserable at those jobs—he later called his *Time* colleagues the "most intelligent and well-informed people I worked with in my life," and said that he put as much creative effort into a *McCall's* promotional campaign as he did into his fiction at night.

Even after the sale of the film rights to *Catch-22* enabled Heller to quit advertising and write full-time, he produced books very slowly; his second novel, *Something Happened,* arrived thirteen years after *Catch-22.* In a 1975 interview he described his process: "I wrote for two or three hours in the morning, then went to a gym to work out. I'd have lunch alone at a counter, go back to the apartment and work some more. Sometimes I'd lie down and just *think* about the book all afternoon—daydream, if you will. In the evenings I'd often go out to dinner with friends."

Heller wrote in longhand on yellow legal pads and reworked passages carefully, often numerous times—by hand and then on a typewriter—before handing them off to a typist for a final copy. "I am a chronic fiddler," he said. While working, he liked to listen to classical music, particularly Bach. And if he skipped a day, he didn't beat himself up. "It's an everyday thing, but I'm never guilt-ridden if I don't work," he said. "I don't have a compulsion to write, and I never have. I have a wish, an ambition to write, but it's not one that justifies the word 'drive.' " Neither was he insecure about his pace of production. "I write very slowly, though if I write a page or two a day five days a week, that's 300 pages a year and it does add up."

James Dickey (1923–1997)

In the late 1950s, Dickey made a brief, reckless foray into the advertising world. He had recently lost a university teaching position and needed a way to make money while he worked on his poetry. With the help of his sister-in-law's neighbor, an executive at the advertising firm McCann Erickson, Dickey landed a job at the firm's Atlanta office, writing radio commercials for Coca-Cola bottlers around the country. It was a demanding position, made more so by the fact that Dickey was simultaneously trying to find time for his literary endeavors during the workday. "Every time I had a minute to spare, which was not often, I would stick a poem in the typewriter where I had been typing Coca-Cola ads," he said. Unlike most of his fellow ad men, Dickey kept his office door shut. If a colleague came knocking, he would quickly clear his desk of poems and poetry books. One colleague remembered Dickey's constant efforts to outsmart his bosses:

> If they said, "Alright, today we need ten television commercials and five radio commercials and two print ads; this is your assignment for the day," he'd say, "OK." He'd shut the door and within an hour he'd have it all done. Then he'd spend the rest of the time working on his own work—his correspondence, his poems. But of course they didn't know that. They figured: "That'll keep him busy all day." But he was so smart and so fast, he could get it all done.

Dickey eventually worked for three Atlanta ad agencies, seeking more senior positions in the hopes that developing big-picture creative campaigns would be less demanding than churning out a constant stream of radio and television ads. Meanwhile, his poetry career was gaining momentum—he had won several significant prizes, and he was working hard to finish a manuscript for publication. By 1961, however, his boss had caught on to the fact that Dickey was more concerned with literature than with advertising, and fired him. Dickey claimed that he had quit; he wrote to a friend, "After five and a half years of working in these dark Satanic mills of American business I am out at last."

Nikola Tesla (1856-1943)

As a young apprentice in Thomas Edison's New York office, Tesla regularly worked from 10:30 in the morning until 5:00 the following morning. ("I've had many hardworking assistants, but you take the cake," Edison told him.) Later, after he had started his own company, Tesla arrived at the office at noon. Immediately, his secretary would draw the blinds; Tesla worked best in the dark and would raise the blinds again only in the event of a lightning storm, which he liked to watch flashing above the cityscape from his black mohair sofa. He typically worked at the office until midnight, with a break at 8:00 for dinner in the Palm Room of the Waldorf-Astoria hotel.

These dinners were carefully scripted affairs. Tesla ate alone, and phoned in his instructions for the meal in advance. Upon arriving, he was shown to his regular table, where eighteen clean linen napkins would be stacked at his place. As he waited for his meal, he would polish the already gleaming silver and crystal with these squares of linen, gradually amassing a heap of discarded napkins on the table. And when his dishes arrived—served to him not by a waiter but by the maître d'hôtel himself—Tesla would mentally calculate their cubic contents before eating, a strange compulsion he had developed in his childhood and without which he could never enjoy his food.

Glenn Gould (1932-1982)

Gould once declared that he was Canada's "most experienced hermit." He was partly joking—the virtuoso pianist liked to feed his reputation as an eccentric genius living in Howard Hughes–ian seclusion in his Toronto apartment. But there was more than a kernel of truth in this depiction. Gould was a zealous hypochondriac, with a range of real and imaginary ailments and a terror of germs (if you sneezed during a telephone call with Gould, he might hang up out of revulsion), and an intensely private person who avoided emotional entanglements and abruptly ended relationships if they became too intimate. From the time he retired from public performances in 1961, when he was thirty-one years old, Gould devoted himself completely to his work, spending the vast majority of his time thinking about music at home or recording music in the studio. He had no hobbies and only a few close friends and collaborators, with whom he communicated mostly by telephone. "I don't think that my life style is like most other people's and I'm rather glad for that," Gould told an interviewer in 1980. "[T]he two things, life style and work, have become one. Now if that's eccentricity, then I'm eccentric."

In another interview, Gould described his preferred schedule:

I tend to follow a very nocturnal sort of existence, mainly because I don't much care for sunlight. Bright colors of any kind depress me, in fact, and my moods are more or less inversely related to the clarity of the sky on any given day. Matter of fact, my private motto has always been that behind every

Glenn Gould, Toronto, the 1970s

silver lining there's a cloud. So I schedule my errands for as late an hour as possible, and I tend to emerge along with the bats and the raccoons at twilight.

Sometimes errands forced him to leave the house earlier, but in general Gould slept until the late afternoon, often making a few phone calls to help himself wake up. Then he might head to the Canadian Broadcasting Centre to collect his mail and catch up on the latest gossip; if he was recording, he would arrive at the studio at about 7:00 P.M. and work there until 1:00 or 2:00 A.M. These recording sessions came with an assortment of familiar (and essential) rituals; as his longtime producer at Columbia Records has written, "for Gould, everything had a routine. It was almost as if the constant repetition of certain rituals created a kind of security blanket." This included periodically soaking his hands in scalding-hot water for twenty minutes, popping the occasional Valium, and sending the piano tuner out for Gould's requisite late-night "double-doubles" (coffees with two sugars and extra cream).

If he wasn't recording, Gould stayed in his apartment as much as possible, to read, make endless to-do lists, study scores, and listen to music. By his own estimate he listened to recordings or the radio for at least six or seven hours a day, and he usually had two radios and the TV all going at the same time, in different rooms. ("I don't approve of people who watch television," he said, "but I am one of them.") His reading habits were similarly voracious: Gould devoured several newspapers a day and a handful of books a week. Surprisingly, he did not spend that much time at the piano—he practiced about an hour a day, sometimes less, and claimed that the "best playing I do is when I haven't touched the instrument for a month."

At 11:00 P.M. Gould began another, longer round of telephone calls, often lasting until 1:00 or 2:00 in the morning. Many of his friends have described the experience of receiving a Gould call: without bothering to ask if it was a good time or making any attempt at preliminary small talk, Gould would launch into whatever was on his mind, chatting away happily for as long as he pleased—sometimes hours—while the receiving party had no choice but to submit to his cheerful, rambling soliloquy. "He was known to read whole essays and books, to sing whole pieces of music over the phone, and several of his musical collaborators have recalled that he even liked to rehearse over the phone, singing through his piano part," Kevin Bazzana writes in *Wondrous Strange: The Life and Art of Glenn Gould.* (Gould's phone bill, Bazzana adds, "routinely ran to four figures.") It was almost impossible to get off the phone with him, although if you fell asleep during the call he probably wouldn't notice.

His phone calls over, Gould would visit a local all-night diner for his sole meal of the day: scrambled eggs, salad, toast, juice, sherbet, and decaf coffee. Eating more frequently made him feel guilty, he said, although he snacked on arrowroot biscuits, Ritz crackers, tea, water, orange juice, and coffee throughout his waking hours. (On recording days he didn't eat at all; fasting, he said, makes the mind sharper.) Finally, at 5:00 or 6:00 A.M., just as the sun was starting to rise, Gould would take a sedative and go to bed.

Louise Bourgeois (1911-2010)

"My life has been regulated by insomnia," Bourgeois told an interviewer in 1993. "It's something that I have never been able to understand, but I accept it." Bourgeois learned to use these sleepless hours productively, propped up in bed with her "drawing diary," listening to music or the hum of traffic on the streets. "Each day is new, so each drawing—with words written on the back—lets me know how I'm doing," she said. "I now have 110 drawing-diary pages, but I'll probably destroy some. I refer to these diaries as 'tender compulsions.' " As for her daylight hours, Bourgeois told another interviewer: "I work like a bee and feel that I accomplish little."

Chester Himes (1909-1984)

"I like to get up early, have a big breakfast, and work at one stretch until it's time for lunch," the American crime novelist said in 1983. "If the mail is good, I generally go on with my writing. If it's bad, my mind is disturbed for the rest of the day. I have nearly always typed my manuscripts, without consulting any reference books or dictionaries. In my hotel room in Paris I only needed cigarettes, a bottle of scotch, and occasionally a good dish of meat and vegetables cooking on the burner behind me. Writing's always whetted my appetite."

Flannery O'Connor (1925-1964)

After being diagnosed with lupus in 1951 and told she would live only another four years, O'Connor returned to her native Georgia and moved in with her mother at the family farm in rural Andalusia. Years earlier, a writing instructor had advised O'Connor to set aside a certain number of hours each day to write, and she had taken his advice to heart; back in Georgia she came to believe, as she wrote to a friend, that "routine is a condition of survival."

A devout Catholic, O'Connor began each day at 6:00 A.M. with morning prayers from her copy of *A Short Breviary*. Then she joined her mother in the kitchen, where they would share a Thermos of coffee while listening to the weather report on the radio. Morning mass was at 7:00, a short drive into town at the Sacred Heart. Her religious obligations fulfilled, O'Connor would turn to her writing, shutting herself away between 9:00 and noon for her daily three hours, which would typically yield three pages—although, she told a reporter, "I may tear it all to pieces the next day."

By the afternoon, O'Connor's energy was spent—the lupus caused her to tire early and experience flulike symptoms and mental fogginess as the day wore on. She passed these hours receiving visitors on the porch and pursuing her hobbies of painting and raising birds—peacocks, which she loved and often incorporated into her stories, as well as ducks, hens, and geese. By sundown she was ready for bed; "I go to bed at nine and am always glad to get there," she wrote. Before bedtime she might recite another prayer from her *Breviary,* but her usual nighttime reading was a seven-hundred-page volume of Thomas Aquinas. "I read a lot of theology because it makes my writing bolder," she said.

William Styron (1925-2006)

"Let's face it, writing is hell," Styron told *The Paris Review* in 1954. "I get a fine warm feeling when I'm doing well, but that pleasure is pretty much negated by the pain of getting started each day." To minimize the pain, Styron evolved an unusual daily routine: he would sleep until noon, then read and think in bed for another hour or so before lunch with his wife at 1:30. In the early afternoon he ran errands and dealt with the mail, then began the slow process of easing into work mode. Listening to music was a key part of this transition: "I often have to play music for an hour in order to feel exalted enough to face the act of composing," he said. By 4:00 he was ready to move to his study for his daily four hours, which would typically yield only about two hundred or three hundred words. At 8:00 he would join his family and friends for cocktails and dinner, after which he would drink, smoke, read, and listen to music until 2:00 or 3:00 in the morning. Styron never drank while writing, but he thought that alcohol was a valuable tool for relaxing the mind and inviting "certain visionary moments" when thinking about the work.

An interviewer once asked Styron if he found that his comfortable, upper-middle-class lifestyle—he lived with his wife and their four children in a pair of large houses in Connecticut and on Martha's Vineyard—had been helpful to his writing, or if it had been confining in some ways. "I think it's been a stabilizing and important influence," Styron replied.

> I could not have lived in Bohemia or lived the life of a renegade or a pariah, but I think my works have been nonetheless revolutionary in their own way and certainly anti-establishment. I have had in my little study in Connecticut all these years that famous line from Flaubert tacked to my wall: "Be regular and orderly in your life like a Bourgeois so that you may be violent and original in your work." I believe it.

Philip Roth (b. 1933)

"Writing isn't hard work, it's a nightmare," Roth said in 1987.

> Coal mining is hard work. This is a nightmare. . . . There's a tremendous uncertainty that's built into the profession, a sustained level of doubt that supports you in some way. A good doctor isn't in a battle with his work; a good writer is locked in a battle with his work. In most professions there's a beginning, a middle, and an end. With writing, it's always beginning again. Temperamentally, we need that

newness. There is a lot of repetition in the work. In fact, one skill that every writer needs is the ability to sit still in this deeply uneventful business.

Roth has cultivated that ability with gusto since at least 1972, when he moved to an austere eighteenth-century house on sixty acres in rural northwest Connecticut. A two-room former guest cottage serves as his studio. He goes there to work each morning after breakfast and exercise. "I write from about 10 till six every day, with an hour out for lunch and the newspaper," he has said. "In the evenings I usually read. That's pretty much it."

For many years he had his second wife, the actress Claire Bloom, as a companion, but since their separation in 1994 he has lived by himself, a condition that seems to suit him. "I live alone, there's no one else to be responsible for or to, or to spend time with," he told David Remnick in 2000.

My schedule is absolutely my own. Usually, I write all day, but if I want to go back to the studio in the evening, after dinner, I don't have to sit in the living room because someone else has been alone all day. I don't have to sit there and be entertaining or amusing. I go back out and I work for two or three more hours. If I wake up at two in the morning—this happens rarely, but it sometimes happens—and something has dawned on me, I turn the light on and I write in the bedroom. I have these little yellow things all over the place. I read till all hours if I want to. If I get up at five and I can't sleep and I want to work, I go out and I go to work. So I work, I'm on call. I'm like a doctor and it's an emergency room. And I'm the emergency.

P. G. Wodehouse (1881-1975)

Wodehouse wrote more than ninety books in his career, continuing to work daily even in his last decade. By then he was living full-time at Remsenburg, the summer retreat on Long Island that he shared with his wife, Ethel, their servants, five cats, and four dogs. In 1971, *The New Yorker*'s Herbert Warren Wind visited Wodehouse at Remsenburg, and noted that the author's two outstanding traits were his industry and his basic cheerfulness. "I seem to be rather good at adjusting to things," Wodehouse said.

The eighty-nine-year-old author rose each day at 7:30 sharp and stepped out onto the back porch for the "daily dozen" series of calisthenic exercises, which he had performed every day since they were introduced in the United States in 1919. Then, his wife still asleep upstairs, Wodehouse fixed himself toast, coffee cake, and tea and, as he ate, read what he called a "breakfast book"— a mystery novel by someone like Ngaio Marsh or Rex Stout, or a light, humorous book. Afterward, he smoked a pipe, took a short walk with the dogs, and, by 9:00, settled down to work. Wind writes:

Wodehouse does his writing in his study—a fairly large, pine-walled room on the ground floor, overlooking the back garden. The principal pieces of furniture are a leather armchair (for lounging and thinking) and a plain wooden desk about three feet by five. On top of the desk are a dictionary, a knife for cleaning out pipes, and a bulky Royal typewriter, which Wodehouse has used since 1934. His method of composition has remained virtually unchanged through the years. He does the first draft in longhand, in pencil. Then he sits down at the Royal and does a moderate amount of revising and polishing as he types. At present, his average output on a good working day is about a thousand words, but when he was younger it was closer to twenty-five hundred. He had his most productive day in 1933, when, to his own astonishment, he knocked off the last eight thousand words of "Thank You, Jeeves." Once, when he was beginning a Wooster-Jeeves novel, he experimented with using a Dictaphone. After he had dictated the equivalent of a page, he played it back to check it over. What he heard sounded so terribly unfunny that he immediately turned off the machine and went back to his pad and pencil.

Lunch at home was followed, at about 2:00, with another walk—Wodehouse's neighbor and longtime friend Guy Bolton would pick him up and they would take an hour's constitutional, with the dogs in tow. Wodehouse had to be back in his study by 3:30 for the soap opera *The Edge of Night,* which he never missed. Then he had a traditional English tea with his wife. After this, according to the biographer Robert McCrum, "he might snooze a bit in his armchair, have a bath, and do some more work, before the evening cocktail (sherry for her, a lethal martini for him) at six, which they took in the sun parlour, overlooking the garden. This was followed by dinner, alone with Ethel, and eaten early to allow the cook to get home to her family. After dinner, Wodehouse would usually read, but occasionally he would play two-handed bridge with Ethel, a habit, he joked, that doubtlessly suggested he was senile."

Edith Sitwell (1887-1964)

Literary legend has it that Sitwell used to lie in an open coffin for a while before she began her day's work; this

Edith Sitwell, 1962

foretaste of the grave was supposed to inspire her maca-
bre fiction and poetry. The tale is probably false. What is
certain is that Sitwell liked to write in bed, beginning at
5:30 or 6:00 A.M., this being "the only time when I can be
sure of quiet." "All women should have a day a week in
bed," Sitwell also remarked, and when she was engrossed
in a writing project she would sometimes stay there all
morning and through the afternoon—until finally, she
said, "I am honestly so tired that all I can do is to lie on
my bed with my mouth open."

Thomas Hobbes (1588–1679)

Hobbes famously described life in the state of nature as
"solitary, poor, nasty, brutish, and short," but the English
philosopher's own experience was very nearly the opposite: he lived a long, productive, and mostly peaceful life,
dying in bed at age ninety-one. He rose each day at about
7:00 A.M., ate a breakfast of bread and butter, and took
his morning walk, meditating as he walked, until 10:00.
Then, returning to his chamber, he would record the
minutes of his thoughts on a sheet of paper pasted to an
inch-thick square lapboard. Dinner was served precisely
at 11:00 A.M. (In his old age, Hobbes gave up wine and
meat, and ate fish daily.) Afterward, he smoked a pipe
and, according to his friend and biographer John Aubrey,
"threw himself immediately on his bed" to nap for half
an hour. In the afternoon, Hobbes wrote in his chamber again, fleshing out his morning notes. In the evening

he would sing a few popular songs in bed before going to sleep—not because he had a good voice but because, Aubrey notes, "he did believe it did his lungs good, and conduced much to prolong his life."

John Milton (1608-1674)

Milton was totally blind for the last twenty years of his life, yet he managed to produce a steady stream of writing, including his magnum opus, the ten-thousand-line epic poem *Paradise Lost,* composed between 1658 and 1664. Milton devoted the morning to solitary contemplation in bed, beginning at 4:00 A.M. (5:00 A.M. in the winter). First he had an aide read to him from the Bible for half an hour. Then Milton was left alone to compose as many lines as his memory could retain. At 7:00, Milton's aide returned to take dictation—and if the aide happened to be running late, one early biographer noted, Milton "would complain, *saying he wanted to be milked.*" After dictation, the aide would read to him until lunch was served at noon. Then Milton walked up and down his garden for three or four hours. In the late afternoon and evening he received visitors, ate a light supper, smoked a pipe, and went to bed at about 9:00.

René Descartes (1596–1650)

Descartes was a late riser. The French philosopher liked to sleep until mid-morning, then linger in bed, thinking and writing, until 11:00 or so. "Here I sleep ten hours every night without being disturbed by any care," Descartes wrote from the Netherlands, where he lived from 1629 until the last few months of his life. "And after my mind has wandered in sleep through woods, gardens, and enchanted palaces where I experience every pleasure imaginable, I awake to mingle the reveries of the night with those of the day." These late-morning hours of meditation constituted his only concentrated intellectual effort for the day; Descartes believed that idleness was essential to good mental work, and he made sure not to overexert himself. After an early lunch, he would take a walk or meet friends for conversation; after supper, he dealt with his correspondence.

This comfortable bachelor's life ended abruptly in late 1649, when Descartes accepted a position in the court of Queen Christina of Sweden, who, at twenty-two, was one of the most powerful monarchs in Europe. It's not entirely clear why he agreed to the appointment. He may have been motivated by a desire for greater recognition and prestige, or by a real interest in shaping the thinking of a young ruler. In any case, it proved a disastrous decision. Arriving in Sweden, in time for one of the coldest winters in memory, Descartes was notified that his lessons to Queen Christina would take place in the mornings—beginning at 5:00 A.M. He had no choice but to obey. But the early hours and bitter cold were too much for him. After only a month on the new schedule, Descartes fell ill, apparently of pneumonia; ten days later he was dead.

Johann Wolfgang von Goethe (1749-1832)

As a young man Goethe could write all day long, but as he grew older he found that he could muster the necessary creative energy only in the mornings. "At one time in my life I could make myself write a printed sheet every day, and I found this quite easy," he said in 1828. "[N]ow I can only work at the second part of my *Faust* in the early hours of the day, when I am feeling revived and strengthened by sleep and not yet harassed by the absurd trivialities of everyday life. And even so, what does this work amount to? If I am very lucky indeed I can manage one page, but as a rule only a hand's-breadth of writing, and often even less if I am in an unproductive mood." These moods were the bane of Goethe's later existence; he thought it futile to try to work without the spark of inspiration. He said, "My advice therefore is that one should not force anything; it is better to fritter away one's unproductive days and hours, or sleep through them, than to try at such times to write something which will give one no satisfaction later on."

Friedrich Schiller (1759-1805)

The German poet, historian, philosopher, and playwright kept a drawer full of rotting apples in his workroom; he said that he needed their decaying smell in order to feel the urge to write. Intolerant of interruptions, Schiller also wrote almost exclusively at night. In the summer he preferred to work outdoors, beside his small garden house in the suburbs of Jena, Germany. An early biographer noted the details of Schiller's nocturnal work periods:

> On his sitting down to his desk at night, he was wont to keep some strong coffee, or wine-chocolate, but more frequently a flask of old Rhenish, or Champagne, standing by him, that he might from time to time repair the exhaustion of nature. Often the neighbours used to hear him earnestly declaiming, in the silence of the night: and whoever had an opportunity of watching him on such occasions, a thing very easy to be done from the heights lying opposite his little garden-house, on the other side of the dell, might see him now speaking aloud and walking swiftly to and fro in his chamber, then suddenly throwing himself down into his chair and writing; and drinking the while, sometimes more than once, from the glass standing near him. In winter he was to be found at his desk till four, or even five o'clock in the morning; in summer, till towards three. He then went to bed, from which he seldom rose till nine or ten.

These long hours of nighttime composition—fueled not only by coffee, wine, chocolate, and the smell of rotting apples but by Schiller's constant smoking and snuff-taking—probably contributed to his sickly constitution and constant physical maladies. Yet Schiller could not abandon the habit; it was the only reliable method to guarantee himself the long, uninterrupted stretches of time he needed to be productive. He wrote to a friend, "We have failed to recognize our great asset: time. A conscientious use of it could make us into something quite amazing."

Franz Schubert (1797-1828)

According to a childhood friend, Schubert "used to sit down at his writing desk every morning at 6 o'clock and compose straight through until 1 o'clock in the afternoon. Meanwhile many a pipe was smoked." The Austrian composer's afternoons were less rigorous; his friend noted, "Schubert never composed in the afternoon; after the midday meal he went to a coffee-house, drank a small portion of black coffee, smoked for an hour or two and read the newspapers at the same time." On summer afternoons, he often went for long walks in the countryside surrounding Vienna, then enjoyed a glass of beer or wine with friends. He avoided giving piano lessons, even though he always needed the money and frequently had to rely on friends for financial support. As one member of his circle remembered, "Schubert was extraordinarily fertile and industrious in composing. For everything else that goes by the name of *work* he had no use."

Franz Liszt (1811-1886)

The Hungarian composer and virtuoso pianist slept little, went to church daily, and smoked and drank constantly. One of his pupils described Liszt's routine:

> He rose at four every morning, even when he had been invited out the previous evening, had drunk a good deal of wine and not got to bed until very late. Soon after rising, and without breakfasting, he went to church. At five he took coffee with me, and with it a couple of dry rolls. Then work began: letters were written or read through, music tried out, and much else. At eight came the post, always bringing a huge pile of items. These were then looked through, personal letters read and answered, or music tried out. . . .
>
> At one o'clock, lunch was brought from the court kitchen when Liszt had not been invited out, which happened very frequently. I often ate with him. The meal was good and substantial, but simple. With it a glass of wine would be drunk, or water and brandy in the French manner, which he liked very much. Then he would smoke—indeed he smoked all the time when not eating or sleeping. Last of all there was the coffee machine. The coffee was burnt freshly every day, something on which Liszt placed great emphasis.

Later in the afternoon, Liszt took a long nap of two hours or more—to make up, in part, for his sleepless nights, which he spent pacing his room and sitting at the piano or writing. Although he drank sparingly at lunch, he continued to drink steadily throughout the afternoon and evening; by his last years he was imbibing one or two bottles of cognac and two or three bottles of wine a day, as well as the occasional glass of absinthe. His contemporaries remember him as having a cheerful disposition, but Liszt obviously had his share of demons. A younger colleague once asked Liszt why he didn't keep a diary. "To live one's life is hard enough," he replied. "Why write down all the misery? It would resemble nothing more than the inventory of a torture chamber."

George Sand (1804–1876)

Sand produced a minimum of twenty manuscript pages nearly every night of her adult life. She always worked late at night, a habit she picked up as a teenager caring for her ailing grandmother, when the nighttime hours were her only chance to be alone and think. As an adult, it was not unusual for her to slip out of a sleeping lover's bed to begin a new novel in the middle of the night. In the mornings, Sand often couldn't remember what she had written during these somnambulant writing sessions. "If I did not have my works on a shelf, I would even forget their titles," she claimed.

Sand's persona was larger than life—there's the famous cross-dressing, the assumption of a male pen name, her numerous affairs with both men and women—but her work habits were fairly austere. She liked to nibble on chunks of chocolate at her desk, and she required regular doses of tobacco (cigars or hand-rolled cigarettes) to stay alert. But she did not subscribe to the idea of the drug-addled artist. She wrote in her autobiography:

> It is said that some artists abuse their need for coffee, alcohol, or opium. I do not really believe that, and if it sometimes amuses them to create under the influence of substances other than their own intoxicating thoughts, I doubt that they kept up such lubrications or showed them off. The work of the imagination is exciting enough, and I confess I have only been able to enhance it with a dash of milk or lemonade, which would hardly qualify me as Byronic. Honestly, I do not believe in a drunk Byron writing beautiful verses. Inspiration can pass through the soul just as easily in the midst of an orgy as in the silence of the woods, but when it is a question of giving form to your thoughts, whether you are secluded in your study or performing on the planks of a stage, you must be in total possession of yourself.

Honoré de Balzac (1799-1850)

Balzac drove himself relentlessly as a writer, motivated by enormous literary ambition as well as a never-ending string of creditors and endless cups of coffee; as Herbert J. Hunt has written, he engaged in "orgies of work punctuated by orgies of relaxation and pleasure." When Balzac was working, his writing schedule was brutal: He ate a light dinner at 6:00 P.M., then went to bed. At 1:00 A.M. he rose and sat down at his writing table for a seven-hour stretch of work. At 8:00 A.M. he allowed himself a ninety-minute nap; then, from 9:30 to 4:00, he resumed work, drinking cup after cup of black coffee. (According to one estimate, he drank as many as fifty cups a day.) At 4:00 P.M. Balzac took a walk, had a bath, and received visitors until 6:00, when the cycle started all over again. "The days melt in my hands like ice in the sun," he wrote in 1830. "I'm not living, I'm wearing myself out in a horrible fashion—but whether I die of work or something else, it's all the same."

Victor Hugo (1802-1885)

When Napoléon III seized control of France in 1851, Hugo was forced into political exile, eventually settling with his family on Guernsey, a British island off the coast of Normandy. In his fifteen years there Hugo would write some of his best work, including three collections of poetry and the novel *Les Misérables*. Shortly after arriving on Guernsey, Hugo purchased Hauteville House—locals believed it was haunted by the ghost of a woman who had committed suicide—and set about making several improvements to the property. Chief among them was an all-glass "lookout" on the roof that resembled a small, furnished greenhouse. This was the highest point on the island, with a panoramic view of the English Channel; on clear days, you could see the coast of France. There Hugo wrote each morning, standing at a small desk in front of a mirror.

He rose at dawn, awakened by the daily gunshot from a nearby fort, and received a pot of freshly brewed coffee and his morning letter from Juliette Drouet, his mistress, whom he had installed on Guernsey just nine doors down from Hauteville House. After reading the passionate words of "Juju" to her "beloved Christ," Hugo swallowed two raw eggs, enclosed himself in his lookout, and wrote until 11:00 A.M. Then he stepped out onto the rooftop and washed from a tub of water left out overnight, pouring the icy liquid over himself and rubbing his body with a horsehair glove. Townspeople passing by could watch the spectacle from the street—as could Juliette, looking out the window of her room.

At noon Hugo headed downstairs for lunch. The biographer Graham Robb writes, "these were the days when prominent men were expected to have opening hours like museums. Hugo welcomed almost everyone, writers collecting snippets for their future memoirs, journalists who came to describe M. Hugo's famous dwelling for their female readers. As the clock struck twelve, he would appear in a grey felt hat and woolen gloves, looking like 'a well-dressed farmer,' and conduct his guests to the dining-room."

Hugo provided handsomely for his guests but ate little himself. After lunch he embarked on a two-hour walk or performed a series of strenuous exercises on the beach. Later he would make his daily visit to the barber (he insisted on keeping the trimmings in an unexplained act of superstition), go for a carriage ride with Juliette, and do more writing at home, often using the afternoon to answer some of the satchel-loads of letters that arrived each day.

As the sun set Hugo spent either a boisterous evening at Juliette's, joined by friends for dinner, conversation, and cards, or a rather gloomy one at home. At family dinners Hugo felt compelled to hold forth on philosophical subjects—pausing only to make sure his wife had not fallen asleep, or to write something down in one of the little notebooks he carried everywhere he went. Hugo's son Charles—one of the three Hugo children who became writers themselves—described the scene: "As soon as he has uttered the slightest ideas—anything other than 'I slept well' or 'Give me something to drink'—he turns away, takes out his notebook and jots down what he has just said. Nothing is lost. Everything ends up in print. When his sons try to use something they heard their father say, they are always caught out. When one of his books appears, they find that all the notes they took have been published."

Charles Dickens (1812-1870)

Dickens was prolific—he produced fifteen novels, ten of which are longer than eight hundred pages, and numerous stories, essays, letters, and plays—but he could not be productive without certain conditions in place. First, he needed absolute quiet; at one of his houses, an extra door had to be installed to his study to block out noise.

And his study had to be precisely arranged, with his writing desk placed in front of a window and, on the desk itself, his writing materials—goose-quill pens and blue ink—laid out alongside several ornaments: a small vase of fresh flowers, a large paper knife, a gilt leaf with a rabbit perched upon it, and two bronze statuettes (one depicting a pair of fat toads dueling, the other a gentleman swarmed with puppies).

Dickens's working hours were invariable. His eldest son recalled that "no city clerk was ever more methodical or orderly than he; no humdrum, monotonous, conventional task could ever have been discharged with more punctuality or with more business-like regularity, than he gave to the work of his imagination and fancy." He rose at 7:00, had breakfast at 8:00, and was in his study by 9:00. He stayed there until 2:00, taking a brief break for lunch with his family, during which he often seemed to be in a trance, eating mechanically and barely speaking a word before hurrying back to his desk. On an ordinary day he could complete about two thousand words in this way, but during a flight of imagination he sometimes managed twice that amount. Other days, however, he would hardly write anything; nevertheless, he stuck to his work hours without fail, doodling and staring out the window to pass the time.

Promptly at 2:00, Dickens left his desk for a vigorous three-hour walk through the countryside or the streets of London, continuing to think of his story and, as he described it, "searching for some pictures I wanted to build upon." Returning home, his brother-in-law remembered, "he looked the personification of energy, which seemed to ooze from every pore as from some hidden reservoir." Dickens's nights, however, were relaxed: he dined at 6:00, then spent the evening with family or friends before retiring at midnight.

Charles Darwin (1809-1882)

When Darwin moved from London to the English countryside in 1842, he did so not just to escape the bustle of city life and raise a family in more peaceful surroundings. He was also harboring a secret—his theory of evolution, which he had formulated in private over the preceding decade but dared not unleash on the public yet. The idea that mankind was descended from beasts would, he knew, be viewed as heretical and arrogant by Victorian society,

An etching of Charles Darwin's study at Down House

and he didn't want to risk personal disgrace and the widespread dismissal of his work. He decided to bide his time at Down House, a former parsonage in an isolated village in Kent—the "extreme edge of [the] world," he called it—where he would live and work for the rest of his life.

From the time he arrived at Down House until 1859, when he finally published *On the Origin of Species,* Darwin led a double life, keeping his thoughts on evolution and natural selection to himself while bolstering his credentials in the scientific community. He became an expert on barnacles, ultimately producing four monographs on the creatures and earning a Royal Medal for his work in 1853. He also studied bees and flowers and wrote books on coral reefs and South American geology. Meanwhile, he divulged his secret theory to a very few confidants; he told one fellow scientist it was "like confessing a murder."

Throughout this time—indeed, for the rest of his life—Darwin's health was poor. He suffered from stomach pains, heart palpitations, severe boils, headaches, and other symptoms; the cause of his illness is unknown, but it seems to have been brought on by overwork during his London years, and it was clearly exacerbated by stress. As a result, Darwin maintained a quiet, monkish life at Down House, with his day structured around a few concentrated bursts of work, broken up by set periods of walking, napping, reading, and letter writing.

The first, and best, of his work periods began at 8:00 A.M., after Darwin had taken a short walk and had a solitary breakfast. Following ninety minutes of focused work in his study—disrupted only by occasional trips to the snuff jar that he kept on a table in the hallway—Darwin met his wife, Emma, in the drawing room to receive the day's post. He read his letters, then lay on the sofa to hear Emma read the family letters aloud. When the letters were done, Emma would continue reading aloud, switching to whatever novel she and her husband were currently working their way through.

At 10:30 Darwin returned to his study and did more work until noon or a quarter after. He considered this the end of his workday, and would often remark in a satisfied voice, "*I've* done a good day's work." Then he took his main walk of the day, accompanied by his beloved fox terrier, Polly. He stopped at the greenhouse first, then made a certain number of laps along the "Sandwalk," striking his iron-shod walking stick rhythmically against the gravel path as he went. Lunch with the family followed. Darwin usually drank a small amount of wine with the meal, which he enjoyed, but very carefully—he had a fear of drunkenness, and claimed to have only ever once been tipsy in his life, while he was a student at Cambridge.

After lunch he returned to the drawing-room sofa to read the newspaper (the only nonscientific literature that he read himself; everything else was read aloud to him). Then it was time for his letter writing, which took place by the fire, in a huge horsehair chair with a board placed across its arms. If he had many letters to write, he would dictate them instead, from a rough copy scrawled across the backs of manuscripts or proofs. Darwin made a point of replying to every letter he received, even those from obvious fools or cranks. If he failed to reply to a single letter, it weighed on his conscience and could even keep him up at night. The letter writing took him until about 3:00 in the afternoon, after which he went upstairs to his bedroom to rest, lying on the sofa with a cigarette while

Emma continued to read from the novel-in-progress. Often Darwin would fall asleep during this reading and, to his dismay, miss chunks of the story.

He came back downstairs at 4:00 to embark on his third walk of the day, which lasted for half an hour, and then returned to his study for another hour of work, tying up any loose ends from earlier in the day. At 5:30, a half-hour of idleness in the drawing room preceded another period of rest and novel reading, and another cigarette, upstairs. Then he joined the family for dinner, although he did not join them in eating the meal; instead, he would have tea with an egg or a small piece of meat. If guests were present, he would not linger at the dinner table to converse with the men, as was customary—even a half-hour of conversation wore him out, and could cause him a sleepless night and the loss of his next day's work. Instead, he joined the ladies in retiring to the drawing room, where he played backgammon with Emma. His son Francis recalls that he "became extremely animated over these games, bitterly lamenting his bad luck and exploding with exaggerated mock-anger at my mother's good fortune."

After two games of backgammon, he would read a scientific book and, just before bed, lie on the sofa and listen to Emma play the piano. He left the drawing room at about 10:00 and was in bed within a half-hour, although he generally had trouble getting to sleep and would often lie awake for hours, his mind working at some problem that he had failed to solve during the day.

Thus his days went for forty years, with few exceptions. He would join his family on summer holidays, and occasionally make short visits to relatives, but he was always relieved to get home and, otherwise, he refrained from making even the most modest public appearances. Despite his seclusion and constant ill health, however, Darwin was content at Down House, surrounded by his family—he and Emma would eventually have ten children—and his work, which seemed to strip the years away from him even as it frequently brought him to the brink of exhaustion. Francis Darwin recalls that his father's slow, labored movements about the house stood in stark contrast to his demeanor during an experiment—then his actions became quick and certain, characterized by a "kind of restrained eagerness. He always gave one the impression of working with pleasure, and not with any drag."

Herman Melville (1819–1891)

Only a few records of Melville's daily routines have survived. Perhaps the best one comes from a December 1850 letter he wrote to a friend shortly after the Melville family moved to Arrowhead, a one-hundred-sixty-acre farm in the Berkshires region of Massachusetts. There, the thirty-one-year-old author raised corn, turnips, potatoes, and pumpkins; he enjoyed working in the fields as a way to relieve the stress of writing six to eight hours a day. Melville wrote:

> I rise at eight—thereabouts—& go to my barn—say good-morning to the horse, & give him his breakfast. (It goes to my heart to give him a cold one, but it can't be helped.) Then, pay a visit to my

cow—cut up a pumpkin or two for her, & stand by to see her eat it—for it's a pleasant sight to see a cow move her jaws—she does it so mildly & with such a sanctity.—My own breakfast over, I go to my work-room & light my fire—then spread my M.S.S. on the table—take one business squint at it, & fall to with a will. At 2½ P.M. I hear a preconcerted knock at my door, which (by request) continues till I rise & go to the door, which serves to wean me effectively from my writing, however interested I may be. My friends the horse & cow now demand their dinner—& I go & give it to them. My own dinner over, I rig my sleigh & with my mother or sisters start off for the village—& if it be a Literary World day, great is the satisfaction thereof. —My evenings I spend in a sort of mesmeric state in my room—not being able to read—only now & then skimming over some large-printed book.

He was by then a few months into *Moby-Dick,* for which his Arrowhead workroom proved an ideal setting. "I have a sort of sea-feeling here in the country, now that the ground is all covered with snow," he wrote. "I look out of my window in the morning when I rise as I would out of a port-hole of a ship in the Atlantic. My room seems a ship's cabin; & at nights when I wake up & hear the wind shrieking, I almost fancy there is too much sail on the house, & I had better go on the roof & rig in the chimney."

Nathaniel Hawthorne (1804-1864)

After graduating from Bowdoin College in 1825, Hawthorne returned home to Salem, Massachusetts, where he embarked on a program of severe literary self-discipline. Shutting himself in his room for most of the day, he read exhaustively and wrote a great deal, although he destroyed much of what he produced. This period from 1825 until 1837, when Hawthorne finally published a collection of short stories, has often been called the "solitary years." The critic Malcolm Cowley describes the writer's habits during this time:

> As the years passed he fell into a daily routine that seldom varied during autumn and winter. Each morning he wrote or read until it was time for the midday dinner; each afternoon he read or wrote or dreamed or merely stared at a sunbeam boring in through a hole in the blind and very slowly moving across the opposite wall. At sunset he went for a long walk, from which he returned late in the evening to eat a bowl of chocolate crumbled thick with bread and then talk about books with his two adoring sisters, Elizabeth and Louisa, both of whom were already marked for spinsterhood; these were almost the only household meetings. . . .
>
> In summer Hawthorne's routine was more varied; he went for an early-morning swim among the rocks and often spent the day wandering alone by the shore, so idly that he amused himself by standing on a cliff and throwing stones at his shadow.

Once, apparently, he stationed himself on the long toll-bridge north of Salem and watched the procession of travelers from morning to night. He never went to church, but on Sunday mornings he liked to stand behind the curtain of his open window and watch the congregation assemble.

After his marriage in 1842, Hawthorne's lifestyle necessarily became less self-centered—although, when he was writing (and he claimed that he could never write during the warm months, only during fall and winter), he still needed several hours of solitude a day. In Concord, where the Hawthornes settled after their marriage, he would stay alone in his study until the early afternoon. "I religiously seclude myself every morning (much against my will)," he wrote to his editor, "and remain in retirement till dinner-time, or thereabouts." Dinner was the midday meal, for which Hawthorne joined his wife at about 2:00. An hour later, he would head into the village to visit the library and the post office. By sunset, he would return home, and his wife would join him for a short walk to the river. They had tea, and then Hawthorne read aloud to her for one or two hours or more.

Leo Tolstoy (1828-1910)

"I must write each day without fail, not so much for the success of the work, as in order not to get out of my routine." This is Tolstoy in one of the relatively few diary entries he made during the mid-1860s, when he was deep into the writing of *War and Peace*. Although he does not describe his routine in the diary, his oldest son, Sergei, later recorded the pattern of Tolstoy's days at Yasnaya Polyana, the family estate in the Tula region of Russia.

> From September to May we children and our teachers got up between eight and nine o'clock and went to the hall to have breakfast. After nine, in his dressing-gown, still unwashed and undressed, with a tousled beard, Father came down from his bedroom to the room under the hall where he finished his toilet. If we met him on the way he greeted us hastily and reluctantly. We used to say: "Papa is in a bad temper until he has washed." Then he, too, came up to have his breakfast, for which he usually ate two boiled eggs in a glass.
>
> He did not eat anything after that until five in the afternoon. Later, at the end of 1880, he began to take luncheon at two or three. He was not talkative at breakfast and soon retired to his study with a glass of tea. We hardly saw him after that until dinner.

According to Sergei, Tolstoy worked in isolation—no one was allowed to enter his study, and the doors to the adjoining rooms were locked to ensure that he would not be interrupted. (An account by Tolstoy's daughter Tatyana disagrees on this point—she remembers that their mother was allowed in the study; she would sit on the divan sewing quietly while her husband wrote.) Before dinner, Tolstoy would go for a walk or a ride, often to supervise some work on the estate grounds. Afterward he rejoined the family in a much more sociable mood. Sergei writes:

> At five we had dinner, to which Father often came late. He would be stimulated by the day's impressions and tell us about them. After dinner he usually read or talked to guests if there were any; sometimes he read aloud to us or saw to our lessons. About 10 P.M. all the inhabitants of [Yasnaya] foregathered again for tea. Before going to sleep he read again, and at one time he played the piano. And then retired to his bed about 1 A.M.

Pyotr Ilich Tchaikovsky (1840-1893)

In 1885, Tchaikovsky rented a dacha in Maidanovo, a small village in the district of Klin, some fifty miles northwest of Moscow. After years of restless wandering through Russia and Europe, the forty-five-year-old composer found his new living arrangement a wonderful relief. "What a joy to be in my own home!" he wrote to his patroness, Nadezhda von Meck. "What a bliss to know that no one will come to interfere with my work, my reading, my walks." He would live in or near Klin for the rest of his life.

Soon after arriving, Tchaikovsky established a daily routine that he followed whenever he was home. He woke early, between 7:00 and 8:00, and gave himself an hour to drink his tea, smoke, and read, first from the Bible, then from some other volume that, his brother, Modest, writes, "was not only pleasure but also work"—a book in English, perhaps, or the philosophy of Spinoza or Schopenhauer. Then he took his first walk of the day, lasting no more than forty-five minutes. At 9:30, Tchaikovsky set to work—composing at the piano only after he had dealt with any proofs or his correspondence, chores that he disliked. "Before setting about the pleasant task," his brother noted, "Pyotr Ilich always hastened to get rid of the unpleasant."

At noon precisely he broke for lunch, which he always enjoyed—the composer was not picky about his food and found virtually every dish excellently prepared, often conveying his compliments to the chef. After lunch he went for a long walk, regardless of the weather. His brother writes, "Somewhere at sometime he had discovered that a man needs a two-hour walk for his health, and his observance of this rule was pedantic and superstitious, as though if he returned five minutes early he would fall ill, and unbelievable misfortunes of some sort would ensue."

Tchaikovsky's superstition may have been justified—his walks were essential to his creativity, and he often stopped to jot down ideas that he would later flesh out at the piano. In a letter to von Meck, Tchaikovsky provided a valuable glimpse of his process.

The seed of a future composition usually reveals itself suddenly, in the most unexpected fashion. If the soil is favourable—that is, if I am in the mood for work, this seed takes root with inconceivable strength and speed, bursts through the soil, puts out roots, leaves, twigs, and finally flowers: I cannot define the creative process except through this metaphor. All the difficulties lie in this: that the seed should appear, and that it should find itself in favourable circumstances. All the rest happens of its own accord. It would be futile for me to try and express to you in words the boundless bliss of that feeling which envelops you when the main idea has appeared, and when it begins to take definite forms. You forget everything, you are almost insane, everything inside you trembles and writhes, you scarcely manage to set down sketches, one idea presses upon another.

After his walk, Tchaikovsky had tea and read the newspaper or historical journals for an hour; then, at 5:00, he put in another two hours of work. Supper was at 8:00. After the meal, if there were guests, Tchaikovsky loved to play cards; if he was alone, he read, played patience, and, his brother notes, "always found himself a little bored."

Mark Twain (1835-1910)

In the 1870s and '80s, the Twain family spent their summers at Quarry Farm in New York, about two hundred miles west of their Hartford, Connecticut, home. Twain found those summers the most productive time for his literary work, especially after 1874, when the farm owners built him a small private study on the property. That same summer, Twain began writing *The Adventures of Tom*

Sawyer. His routine was simple: he would go to the study in the morning after a hearty breakfast and stay there until dinner at about 5:00. Since he skipped lunch, and since his family would not venture near the study—they would blow a horn if they needed him—he could usually work uninterruptedly for several hours. "On hot days," he wrote to a friend, "I spread the study wide open, anchor my papers down with brickbats, and write in the midst of the hurricane, clothed in the same thin linen we make shirts of."

After dinner, Twain would read his day's work to the assembled family. He liked to have an audience, and his evening performances almost always won their approval. On Sundays, Twain skipped work to relax with his wife and children, read, and daydream in some shady spot on the farm. Whether or not he was working, he smoked cigars constantly. One of his closest friends, the writer William Dean Howells, recalled that after a visit from Twain, "the whole house had to be aired, for he smoked all over it from breakfast to bedtime." Howells also records Twain's difficulties getting to sleep at night:

> In those days he was troubled with sleeplessness, or, rather, with reluctant sleepiness, and he had various specifics for promoting it. At first it had been champagne just before going to bed, and we provided that, but later he appeared from Boston with four bottles of lager-beer under his arms; lager-beer, he said now, was the only thing to make you go to sleep, and we provided that. Still later, on a visit I paid him at Hartford, I learned that hot Scotch was the only soporific worth considering, and Scotch

whiskey duly found its place on our sideboard. One day, very long afterward, I asked him if he were still taking hot Scotch to make him sleep. He said he was not taking anything. For a while he had found going to bed on the bath-room floor a soporific; then one night he went to rest in his own bed at ten o'clock, and he had gone promptly to sleep without anything. He had done the like with the like effect ever since. Of course, it amused him; there were few experiences of life, grave or gay, which did not amuse him, even when they wronged him.

Alexander Graham Bell (1847-1922)

As a young man, Bell tended to work around the clock, allowing himself only three or four hours of sleep a night. After his marriage and his wife's pregnancy, however, the American inventor was persuaded to keep more regular hours. His wife, Mabel, forced him to get out of bed for breakfast each morning at 8:30 A.M.—"It is hard work and tears are spent over it sometimes," she noted in a letter—and convinced him to reserve a few work-free hours after they dined together at 7:00 P.M. (He was allowed to return to his study at 10:00.)

Once he got adjusted to it, Bell found that his new family-friendly schedule agreed with him—but he couldn't keep it up indefinitely. When in the throes of a new idea, he pleaded with his wife to let him be free of family obligations; sometimes, in these states, he would work for up to twenty-two hours straight without sleep. According to

Mabel's journal, Bell explained to her that "I have my periods of restlessness when my brain is crowded with ideas tingling to my fingertips when I am excited and cannot stop for anybody." Mabel eventually accepted his relentless focus on his work, but not without some resentment. She wrote to him in 1888, "I wonder do you think of me in the midst of that work of yours of which I am so proud and yet so jealous, for I know it has stolen from me part of my husband's heart, for where his thoughts and interests lie, there must his heart be."

Vincent van Gogh (1853-1890)

"Today again from seven o'clock in the morning till six in the evening I worked without stirring except to take some food a step or two away," van Gogh wrote in an 1888 letter to his brother, Theo, adding, "I have no thought of fatigue, I shall do another picture this very night, and I shall bring it off." This seems to have been typical for the artist; when in the grip of creative inspiration, van Gogh painted nonstop, "in a dumb fury of work," barely pausing to eat. And when his friend and fellow painter Paul Gauguin came to visit a few months later, van Gogh's habits scarcely changed. He wrote to Theo, "Our days pass in working, working all the time, in the evening we are dead beat and go off to the café, and after that, early to bed! Such is our life."

N. C. Wyeth (1882-1945)

The American painter and illustrator woke at 5:00 A.M. every day and chopped wood until 6:30. Then, "fortified by grapefruit, eggs, pancakes, and coffee," the biographer David Michaelis writes, Wyeth climbed the hill to his studio. Before painting he liked to settle his breakfast by writing a letter, which he often mailed right away, driving to the village post office in his station wagon. On the way back, he would look in on a painting student, sometimes taking up the brush himself for a "working criticism."

Back at his studio, Wyeth donned a smock, stuck a pipe between his teeth, hooked a giant palette onto his left thumb, and set to work, pacing in front of his easel in between rapid brushstrokes. He worked fast, sometimes completing an entire painting in only a few hours. If the work wasn't going well, Wyeth would tape a piece of cardboard to the side of his glasses, blocking his view of the studio's large north window in an effort to improve his concentration. When he broke for lunch at 1:00, he would sometimes forget to remove this makeshift blinder—a sure sign to his family that the work was going poorly and he would be in a bad temper.

Generally, however, Wyeth was happy as long as he was painting—and his children were welcome to join him in the studio in the afternoons, playing among themselves while he continued to paint in silence. Wyeth almost never worked under artificial light, so the daylight hours were precious to him. He hated to stop at the end of the day, often wishing he could start the next day immediately. "It's the hardest work in the world to try *not* to work!" he said.

Georgia O'Keeffe (1887-1986)

"I like to get up when the dawn comes," O'Keeffe told an interviewer in 1966. "The dogs start talking to me and I like to make a fire and maybe some tea and then sit in bed and watch the sun come up. The morning is the best time, there are no people around. My pleasant disposition likes the world with nobody in it." Living in the New Mexico desert, which she made her permanent home from 1949 until her death, O'Keeffe had no trouble finding the solitude that she craved. Most days she took a half-hour walk in the early morning, keeping an eye out for rattlesnakes on her property, which she would kill with her walking stick (she kept their rattles in a box to show to visitors). Then there would be breakfast at 7:00, prepared by O'Keeffe's cook—a typical meal included hot chili with garlic oil, soft-boiled or scrambled eggs, bread with a savory jam, sliced fresh fruit, and coffee or tea. If she was painting, O'Keeffe would then work in her studio for the rest of the day, breaking at noon for lunch. If she wasn't painting, she would work in the garden, do housework, answer letters, and receive visitors. But the painting days were the best days, O'Keeffe said:

> On the other days one is hurrying through the other things one imagines one has to do to keep one's life

going. You get the garden planted. You get the roof fixed. You take the dog to the vet. You spend a day with a friend. . . . You may even enjoy doing such things. . . . But always you are hurrying through these things with a certain amount of aggravation so that you can get at the paintings again because that is the high spot—in a way it is what you do all the other things for. . . . The painting is like a thread that runs through all the reasons for all the other things that make one's life.

O'Keeffe's last meal of the day was a light supper at 4:30 in the afternoon—she ate early in order to leave plenty of time for an evening drive through her beloved countryside. "When I think of death," she once said, "I only regret that I will not be able to see this beautiful country anymore."

Sergey Rachmaninoff (1873-1943)

"Some pianists say they are the slaves of their instrument," Rachmaninoff told a reporter in 1933. "If I am its slave, all I can say is—I have a very kind master." Two hours a day was all the practice he needed to stay in top form. Composing, however, was a different matter—Rachmaninoff could never seem to find as much uninterrupted time as he needed. As he wrote to a friend in 1907, "today I worked only from 9 A.M. to 12:30. Then lunch, and now I write you instead of working. I have one free hour and then an hour's walk. Then 2 hours' practice, and then I retire with the chickens. Thus I have only about 4 hours a day for composition. Too little!"

Vladimir Nabokov (1899-1977)

The Russian-born novelist's writing habits were famously peculiar. Beginning in 1950, he composed first drafts in pencil on ruled index cards, which he stored in long file boxes. Since, Nabokov claimed, he pictured an entire novel in complete form before he began writing it, this method allowed him to compose passages out of sequence, in whatever order he pleased; by shuffling the cards around, he could quickly rearrange paragraphs, chapters, and whole swaths of the book. (His file box also served as portable desk; he started the first draft of *Lolita* on a road trip across America, working nights in the backseat of his parked car—the only place in the country, he said, with no noise and no drafts.) Only after months of this labor did he finally relinquish the cards to his wife, Vera, for a typed draft, which would then undergo several more rounds of revisions.

As a young man, Nabokov preferred to write in bed while chain-smoking, but as he grew older (and quit smoking) his habits changed. He described his routine in a 1964 interview: "I generally start the day at a lovely old-fashioned lectern I have in my study. Later on, when I feel gravity nibbling at my calves, I settle down in a comfortable armchair alongside an ordinary writing desk; and finally, when gravity begins climbing up my spine,

I lie down on a couch in a corner of my small study." By this time he had settled with his wife in a six-room apartment at the top floor of the Palace Hotel, in Montreux, Switzerland, where he could look down on Lake Geneva from his lectern. In the same interview, Nabokov elaborated on his daily schedule:

> I awake around seven in winter: my alarm clock is an Alpine chough—big, glossy, black thing with big yellow beak—which visits the balcony and emits a most melodious chuckle. For a while I lie in bed mentally revising and planning things. Around eight: shave, breakfast, enthroned meditation, and bath—in that order. Then I work till lunch in my study, taking time out for a short stroll with my wife along the lake. . . . We lunch around one P.M., and I am back at my desk by half-past one and work steadily till half-past six. Then a stroll to a news-stand for the English papers, and dinner at seven. No work after dinner. And bed around nine. I read till half-past eleven, and then tussle with insomnia till one A.M.

"My habits are simple, my tastes banal," he later wrote. His keenest pleasures were "soccer matches on the TV, an occasional cup of wine or a triangular gulp of canned beer, sunbaths on the lawn, and composing chess problems." And, of course, pursuing his beloved butterflies, which he did in summer on the Alpine slopes, often hiking fifteen miles or more a day—after which, he grumpily noted, "I sleep even worse than in winter."

Balthus (1908-2001)

The enigmatic painter published his first book at age twelve—it contained forty drawings illustrating a story about a cat by Rainer Maria Rilke, his mother's lover at

Balthus's studio in Rossinière, Switzerland, 1990

the time—and he continued to paint daily into his eighties. By then, the self-styled Count Balthus Klossowski de Rola had ensconced himself in a palatial chalet in the Swiss Alps, where he lived a life of aristocratic refinement surrounded by his wife, his servants, and his cats.

After a 9:30 breakfast and the reading of the mail, Balthus studied the light conditions of the morning. "This is the one way to know if you will paint today, if the progress into the painting's mystery will be intense," he said. In the late morning or just after lunch, Balthus would head to his studio on the outskirts of the nearby village—walking with the aid of a cane or, later, being pushed in a wheelchair by his wife, Setsuko. His painting day always began with a prayer, followed by hours of meditation in front of the canvas. Sometimes he would spend an entire session like this, without even adding a brushstroke. Smoking was essential to this state:

> I've always painted while smoking. I am reminded of this habit in photographs from my youth. I intuitively understood that smoking doubled my faculty of concentration, allowing me to be entirely within a canvas. Now that my body is weaker, I smoke less, but I wouldn't miss for anything the exquisite moments of contemplation before a painting-in-progress, with a cigarette between my lips, helping me to advance into it. There are also happy moments spent smoking after meals or tea; the Countess always places cigarettes on a little night table next to the table where I eat lunch. It's a great moment of happiness, what Baudelaire called, I believe, "the pleasant hours."

At 4:30 or 5:00, Balthus returned to the chalet and joined his wife for a traditional tea service, with jams, fruitcake, and chocolate tarts. After an 8:00 supper, they often settled in the library to watch movies on a wide-screen television. Balthus particularly liked action films, Westerns, and operas.

Le Corbusier (1887-1965)

The Swiss architect Charles-Édouard Jeanneret—who reinvented himself as Le Corbusier in the early 1920s—maintained a rigid schedule throughout his professional life, yet it was hardly a punishing one. After waking at 6:00 A.M., he did forty-five minutes of calisthenics. Then he served his wife her morning coffee and, at 8:00, the couple ate breakfast together. The rest of Corbusier's morning was devoted to painting, drawing, and writing. This was the most creative part of his day, and even though he often spent hours on paintings that had no direct relation to his architecture, and which he showed to no one other than his wife, he attributed his professional success to these private mornings of artistic contemplation.

Le Corbusier's office hours were brief. He arrived at the studio (a short subway or taxi ride from home) at 2:00 P.M. sharp, and put his employees to work on the ideas he had come up with during the morning. He usually returned home by 5:30, although he occasionally lost track of time. An associate remembers:

The process of returning home revealed quite a lot about Le Corbusier's character. If the work went well, if he enjoyed his own sketching and was sure of what he intended to do, then he forgot about the hour and might be home late for dinner. But if things did not go too well, if he felt uncertain of his ideas and unhappy with his drawings, then Corbu became jittery. He would fumble with his wristwatch—a small, oddly feminine contraption, far too small for his big paw—and finally say, grudgingly, "C'est difficile, l'architecture," toss the pencil or charcoal stub on the drawing, and slink out, as if ashamed to abandon the project and me—and us—in a predicament.

Buckminster Fuller (1895-1983)

The American architect and inventor (he called himself a "comprehensive, anticipatory design scientist") was frequently his own research subject as well (he also called himself Guinea Pig B). Just as he questioned humans' accepted modes of living and transportation—popularizing the geodesic dome and prototyping the three-wheeled, blimp-shaped Dymaxion vehicle, among other futuristic inventions—he also eschewed traditional models of behavior. In the early 1930s, it occurred to Bucky (as everyone called him) that ingrained human sleep patterns might no longer be practical for modern lifestyles. He figured that if he could train himself to sleep less, he could have vastly more time to work. J. Baldwin describes the resulting experiment in "high-frequency sleep":

> A series of trials in 1932 and 1933 convinced him that feeling tired or sleepy was a sign that he had already overtaxed his body and mind to the point where they *had* to rest and recuperate. He decided to try deliberately sleeping before that point arrived. If he slept before pushing himself to exhaustion, repair and recuperation might not be necessary. Sleep would be for rest only. Perhaps it could be brief. If he kept to a certain routine, perhaps he would never be tired.
>
> After trying many schemes, Bucky found a schedule that worked for him: He catnapped for approximately thirty minutes after each six hours of work; sooner if signaled by what he called "broken fixation of interest." It worked (for him). I can personally attest that many of his younger colleagues and students could not keep up with him. He never seemed to tire. His lectures could go on for ten hours or more. He seemed to be always scribbling notes, reading, making models, or just prowling around. The ability to keep going in that manner continued undiminished well into his 70s.

Baldwin writes that Fuller also "disconcerted observers by going to sleep in thirty seconds, as if he had thrown an Off switch in his head. It happened so quickly that it looked like he had had a seizure." Nevertheless, despite the apparent success of his high-frequency-sleep experiment, Fuller did not stick with it indefinitely; eventually his wife complained of his odd hours, and Bucky went back to a more normal schedule, although he continued to take catnaps during the day as needed.

Paul Erdős (1913-1996)

Erdős was one of the most brilliant and prolific mathematicians of the twentieth century. He was also, as Paul Hoffman documents in his book *The Man Who Loved Only Numbers,* a true eccentric—a "mathematical monk" who lived out of a pair of suitcases, dressed in tattered suits, and gave away almost all the money he earned, keeping just enough to sustain his meager lifestyle; a hopeless bachelor who was extremely (perhaps abnormally) devoted to his mother and never learned to cook or even boil his own water for tea; and a fanatic workaholic who routinely put in nineteen-hour days, sleeping only a few hours a night.

Erdős liked to work in short, intense collaborations with other mathematicians, and he crisscrossed the globe seeking fresh talent, often camping out in colleagues' homes while they worked on a problem together. One such colleague remembered an Erdős visit from the 1970s:

> . . . he only needed three hours of sleep. He'd get up early and write letters, mathematical letters. He'd sleep downstairs. The first time he stayed, the clock was set wrong. It said 7:00, but it was really 4:30 A.M. He thought we should be up working, so he

turned on the TV full blast. Later, when he knew me better, he'd come up at some early hour and tap on the bedroom door. "Ralph, do you exist?" The pace was grueling. He'd want to work from 8:00 A.M. until 1:30 A.M. Sure we'd break for short meals but we'd write on napkins and talk math the whole time. He'd stay a week or two and you'd collapse at the end.

Erdős owed his phenomenal stamina to amphetamines—he took ten to twenty milligrams of Benzedrine or Ritalin daily. Worried about his drug use, a friend once bet Erdős that he wouldn't be able to give up amphetamines for a month. Erdős took the bet and succeeded in going cold turkey for thirty days. When he came to collect his money, he told his friend, "You've showed me I'm not an addict. But I didn't get any work done. I'd get up in the morning and stare at a blank piece of paper. I'd have no ideas, just like an ordinary person. You've set mathematics back a month." After the bet, Erdős promptly resumed his amphetamine habit, which he supplemented with shots of strong espresso and caffeine tablets. "A mathematician," he liked to say, "is a machine for turning coffee into theorems."

Andy Warhol (1928–1987)

Every weekday morning from 1976 until his death in 1987, Warhol spoke on the phone to his longtime friend and writing collaborator Pat Hackett and related the

Andy Warhol, circa 1981

events of the previous twenty-four hours—the people he'd seen, the money he'd spent, the gossip he'd heard, the parties he'd attended. Hackett took notes during the calls, which typically lasted one to two hours, and then typed up the accounts in diary form. The diary was initially kept for tax purposes—Warhol detailed all of his cash expenditures, and the typed pages were later stapled to his weekly receipts—but it became something more, an intimate portrait of an artist rarely given to intimacy. In her introduction to *The Andy Warhol Diaries,* published in abridged form in 1989, Hackett describes Warhol's daily routine in the late seventies and eighties:

> Keeping to his beloved weekday "rut" was so important to Andy that he veered from it only when he was forced to. After "doing the Diary" with me on the

phone, he'd make or take a few more phone calls, shower, get dressed, take his cherished dachshunds Archie and Amos into the elevator with him and go from the third floor of his house, where his bedroom was, to the basement kitchen where he'd have break-fast with his two Filipina housekeepers, sisters Nina and Aurora Bugarin. Then he'd tuck some copies of *Interview* under his arm and go out shopping for a few hours, usually along Madison Avenue, then in the auction houses, the jewelry district around 47th Street, and the Village antique shops. He'd pass out the magazine to shopkeepers (in the hope that they would decide to advertise) and to fans who recog-nized him in the street and stopped him—he felt good always having something to *give* them.

He'd get to the office between one and three o'clock, depending on whether there was a busi-ness advertising lunch there or not. Upon arrival he'd reach into his pocket—or his boot—for some cash and send one of the kids out to Brownies down the block for snacks. Then while he was drinking his carrot juice or tea he'd check the appointment books for that afternoon's and night's events, return calls, and take some of the calls that came in as he was standing there. He would also open the stacks of mail he got every day, deciding just which letters, invitations, gifts, and magazines to drop into a "Time Capsule," meaning one of the hun-dreds of 10x18x14-inch brown cardboard boxes, which would be sealed, dated, put into storage, and instantly replaced with an identical empty box. Less than one percent of all the items that he was constantly being sent or given did he keep for himself or give away. All the rest were "for the box": things he considered "interesting," which to Andy, who was interested in everything, meant literally everything. . . .

He'd stay in the main reception area for an hour or two talking to people around the office about their love-lives, diets, and where they'd gone the night before. Then he'd move to the sunny window ledge by the phones and read the day's newspapers, leaf through magazines, take a few more random phone calls, talk a little business with Fred and Vincent [Hughes and Fremont, Warhol's manager and general office manager]. Eventually he'd go to his working area in the back part of the loft near the freight elevator and there he would paint, draw, cut, move images around, etc., until the end of the day when he would sit down with Vincent and pay bills and talk on the phone to friends, locking in the night's itinerary.

Between six and seven o'clock, once the rush-hour traffic was over, he'd walk over to Park Avenue and get a cab uptown. He'd spend a few minutes at home doing what he called "gluing"—washing his face, adjusting the silver "hair" that was his trademark, and maybe, *maybe* changing his clothes, but only if it was an especially "heavy" evening. Then he'd check to make sure there was film in his instant camera. (From the mid-sixties to the mid-seventies, Andy was notorious for endlessly tape-recording his friends. But by the end of the seventies he'd gotten bored with random taping and usually would record people only for a specific reason—that is, if he felt he could use what they said as dialogue for a play or movie script.) Then he'd leave for the night—sometimes to multiple dinners and parties, sometimes just to an early movie and dinner. But no matter how late he stayed out, he was always ready for the Diary again early the next morning.

Edward Abbey (1927-1989)

"When I'm writing a book I pack a lunchbox every morning, retire to my shack down by the wash and hide for four or five hours," the American environmentalist and essayist wrote in 1981, in reply to a fan's inquiries about his working habits. "Between books I take vacations that tend to linger on for months. Indolence-and-melancholy then becomes my major vice, until I get back to work. A writer must be hard to live with: when not working he is miserable, and when he is working he is obsessed. Or so it is with me." Abbey typically warmed up for a morning of writing by lighting his corncob pipe and firing off a letter or two. He did not particularly like settling down to work. "I hate commitments, obligations and working under pressure," he wrote to his editor. "But on the other hand, I like getting paid in advance and I only work under pressure."

V. S. Pritchett (1900-1997)

"Pritchett was a serious imaginative artist," Jeremy Treglown notes in his 2004 biography, "but first and foremost he was a professional writer, one who took intense pride in managing to support himself as that." To do so, the British essayist and short-story writer maintained a routine of unfailing regularity. Mornings he dawdled a little on the way to the writing desk, fixing a pot of tea for himself and his wife at 7:00 or 7:30, and taking it back to bed with the daily papers. After a first pass at the *Times* crossword puzzle, he would return to the kitchen to prepare his own breakfast—the only meal he cooked, usually consisting of bacon, eggs, and burnt toast—and make a second pot of tea for his wife. Following a bath, Pritchett finally "clocked on" to work in his study, a steep climb to the fourth floor of the house, far from the noise of the London streets below.

His first ritual was to light a pipe, and as the day wore on he would surround himself with spent matches. Pritchett wrote longhand on an old pastry board arranged across the arms of his desk chair, his papers held in place by a binder clip. He would write all morning, breaking at about 1:00 for a martini and lunch downstairs. After another look at the crossword, he napped for an hour or so in the library, made more tea, and ran errands in the neighborhood. He could usually fit in two more hours of work before supper at 7:00; and, often, the hours between supper and bed were occupied by another round of work.

Edmund Wilson (1895-1972)

According to the biographer Lewis M. Dabney, "Wilson was the only well-known literary alcoholic of his generation whose work was not compromised by his drinking." And Wilson could certainly drink. The literary critic and essayist readily imbibed whatever was on offer, including bathtub gin and even pure alcohol, although he preferred Molson beer and Johnnie Walker Red Label. The poet Stephen Spender recalled that "at the Princeton Club he would order six martinis and drink them one after another." Nevertheless, Wilson rarely had a hangover, and he could get by on little sleep. He always resumed work at 9:00 in the morning and continued, pausing only to eat lunch at his desk, until 3:00 or 4:00 in the afternoon. "You have to set a goal for each day and stick to it," he said. "I usually try to do six pages." (These were legal-sized sheets written in pencil, and he later upped the quota to seven pages.)

The heavy drinking came later in the evening, but Wilson was not against taking an occasional slug of whiskey to help him start or finish a troublesome piece. On top of his daily six or seven pages, he found time to reply to letters and write in his journal, where, in addition to working out ideas for his fiction and essays, he recorded, in clinical detail, blow-by-blow accounts of his sexual relations with the women in his life. (Wilson had four wives and countless affairs, and managed to exert a strong appeal to women despite his pudgy physical unattractiveness.) He refused to spend time writing about things he did not care about—and although he struggled to stay afloat financially for his entire life, Wilson was proud that he could make a living writing only about that which genuinely interested him. "To write what you are interested in writing and to succeed in getting editors to pay for it," he noted, "is a feat that may require pretty close calculation and a good deal of ingenuity."

John Updike (1932-2009)

"I would write ads for deodorants or labels for catsup bottles, if I had to," Updike told *The Paris Review* in 1967. "The miracle of turning inklings into thoughts and thoughts into words and words into metal and print and ink never palls for me." For much of his career, Updike rented a small office above a restaurant in downtown Ipswich, Massachusetts, where he would write for three or four hours each morning, netting about three pages per day. "Around noon the smell of food would start to rise through the floor, but I tried to hold out another hour before I tumbled downstairs, dizzy with cigarettes, to order a sandwich," Updike later recalled. In a 1978 interview, he described his routine in more detail:

> I try to write in the morning and then into the afternoon. I'm a later riser; fortunately, my wife is also a late riser. We get up in unison and fight for the newspaper for half an hour. Then I rush into my office around 9:30 and try to put the creative project first. I have a late lunch, and then the rest of the day somehow gets squandered. There is a great deal of

busywork to a writer's life, as to a professor's life, a great deal of work that matters only in that, if you don't do it, your desk becomes very full of papers. So, there is a lot of letter answering and a certain amount of speaking, though I try to keep that at a minimum. But I've never been a night writer, unlike some of my colleagues, and I've never believed that one should wait until one is inspired because I think that the pleasures of not writing are so great that if you ever start indulging them you will never write again. So, I try to be a regular sort of fellow—much like a dentist drilling his teeth every morning—except Sunday, I don't work on Sunday, and there are of course some holidays I take.

He told another interviewer that he was careful to give at least three hours a day to the writing project at hand; otherwise, he said, there was a risk he might forget what it's about. A solid routine, he added, "saves you from giving up."

Albert Einstein (1879-1955)

Einstein immigrated to the United States in 1933, where he held a professorship at Princeton University until his retirement in 1945. His routine there was simple. Between 9:00 and 10:00 A.M. he ate breakfast and perused the daily papers. At about 10:30 he left for his Princeton office, walking when the weather was nice; otherwise, a station wagon from the university would pick him up. He worked until 1:00, then returned home for a 1:30 lunch, a nap, and a cup of tea. The rest of the afternoon was spent at home, continuing his work, seeing visitors, and dealing with the correspondence that his secretary had sorted earlier in the day. Supper was at 6:30, followed by more work and more letters.

Despite his humble lifestyle, Einstein was a celebrity in Princeton, famous not only for his scientific accomplishments but also for his absentmindedness and disheveled appearance. (Einstein wore his hair long to avoid visits to the barber and eschewed socks and suspenders, which he considered unnecessary.) Walking to and from work, he was often waylaid by locals who wanted to meet the great physicist. A colleague remembered: "Einstein would pose with the waylayer's wife, children, or grandchildren as desired and exchange a few good-humored words. Then he would go on, shaking his head, saying: 'Well, the old elephant has gone through his tricks again.' "

L. Frank Baum (1856-1919)

In 1910, the author of *The Wonderful Wizard of Oz*—as well as an eventual thirteen Oz sequels and dozens of other fantasy stories and novels—moved from Chicago to Hollywood, where he and his wife bought a corner lot and built a large, comfortable house that they dubbed Ozcot. There, Baum divided his time between writing and a new passion, gardening, which he studied carefully, eventually raising a prize-winning assortment of flowers in the backyard.

At Ozcot, Baum would get up at about 8:00 and eat a hearty breakfast, accompanied by four or five cups of strong coffee with cream and sugar. Following breakfast, he would change into his work clothes and devote the remainder of the morning to his flowers. Lunch was at 1:00, and only after that did Baum turn to his writing— and even then, not always for long. He liked to compose in a garden chair, a cigar in his mouth, writing longhand on a clipboard. Often, however, he would end up back in the flower beds, puttering about while he tried to work out ideas for the book. "My characters just won't do what I want them to," he would explain.

Knut Hamsun (1859-1952)

In a 1908 letter to a potential translator, the Norwegian author provided a glimpse of his creative process:

> A great deal of what I have written has come in the night, when I have slept for a couple of hours and then woken up. I am clear-headed then, and acutely impressionable. I always have a pencil and paper by my bed, I do not use light, but start writing immediately in the dark if I feel something is streaming through me. It has become a habit and I have no difficulty in deciphering my writing in the morning.

As Hamsun grew older and became an increasingly light sleeper, he would often slip into a half-doze for large parts of the day. To compensate for his lack of energy, he would seize on whatever flashes of inspiration came to him, scribbling them down immediately on scraps of paper. Later, he would spread his slips of paper out on a table, sifting through them for clues to a story or character.

Willa Cather (1873-1947)

In 1921, an editor of the *Bookman* visited Cather in her Greenwich Village apartment to discuss the author's recent publications—which included a new collection of short stories and, a few years earlier, the third of her "Prairie Trilogy" novels, *My Ántonia*—as well as her writing routine and habits. "I work from two and a half to three hours a day," Cather told him.

> I don't hold myself to longer hours; if I did, I wouldn't gain by it. The only reason I write is because it interests me more than any other activity I've ever found. I like riding, going to operas and concerts, travel in the west; but on the whole writing interests me more than anything else. If I made a chore of it, my enthusiasm would die. I make it an adventure every day. I get more entertainment from it than any I could buy, except the privilege of hearing a few great musicians and singers. To listen to them interests me as much as a good morning's work.
>
> For me the morning is the best time to write. During the other hours of the day I attend to my housekeeping, take walks in Central Park, go to

concerts, and see something of my friends. I try to keep myself fit, fresh; one has to be in as good form to write as to sing. When not working, I shut work from my mind.

Ayn Rand (1905-1982)

In 1942, under pressure to finish what would become her breakthrough novel, *The Fountainhead,* Rand turned to a doctor to help her overcome her chronic fatigue. He prescribed Benzedrine, still a relatively new drug at the time, to boost her energy levels. It did the trick. According to the biographer Anne C. Heller, Rand had spent years planning and composing the first third of her novel; over the next twelve months, fueled by Benzedrine pills, she averaged a chapter a week. Her writing routine during this period was grueling: she wrote day and night, sometimes neglecting to go to bed for days (she took naps on the couch in her clothes instead). At one point she worked for thirty hours straight, pausing only to eat the meals prepared by her husband or to read him a new passage and discuss bits of dialogue. Even when she got stuck, Rand stayed at her desk. A typist who later worked with Rand recalled her habits:

> She was very disciplined. She seldom left her desk. If she had a problem with the writing—if she had what she called the "squirms"—she solved the problem at her desk; she didn't get up and pace around the apartment, or wait for inspiration, or turn on

the radio or television. She wasn't writing every minute. Once I heard a flapping sound coming from the study—she was playing solitaire. She might read the newspaper. At times, I entered the study to find her sitting with her elbows on the desk and resting her chin on her hands, looking out the window, smoking, thinking.

The Benzedrine helped Rand push through the last stages of *The Fountainhead*, but it soon became a crutch. She would continue to use amphetamines for the next three decades, even as her overuse led to mood swings, irritability, emotional outbursts, and paranoia—traits Rand was susceptible to even without drugs.

George Orwell (1903-1950)

In 1934, Orwell found himself in a typical bind for an aspiring young writer. Despite having published his first book the year before—the generally well received *Down and Out in Paris and London*—Orwell couldn't support himself on his writing alone. But the lowly teaching jobs he had been holding left him little time to write and put him on the margins of literary society. Luckily, Orwell's Aunt Nellie found him an attractive alterative: a part-time assistant job at a London secondhand bookshop.

The post at Booklovers' Corner proved an ideal fit for the thirty-one-year-old bachelor. Waking at 7:00, Orwell went to open the shop at 8:45 and stayed there for an hour. Then he had free time until 2:00, when he would return to the shop and work until 6:30. This left him almost four and a half hours of writing time in the morning and early afternoon, which, conveniently, were the times that he was most mentally alert. And with his writing day behind him, he could happily yawn through the long afternoons in the shop and look forward to free time in the evening—spent sauntering around the neighborhood or, later, hovering over a new purchase: a small gas stove known as the Bachelor Griller, which could grill, boil, and fry, and that allowed Orwell to modestly entertain guests at his small flat.

James T. Farrell (1904–1979)

By the 1950s, the consensus in the literary world was that Farrell's best work was behind him; the novelist was revered for the *Studs Lonigan* trilogy, published two decades earlier, but his later works had made little impression. Farrell, however, wasn't willing to fade into obscurity. In 1958, he embarked on his most ambitious project yet, a multi-novel cycle (he originally estimated it at three to seven books, but in one interview bragged that it would run to at least twenty-five volumes) called *The Universe of Time*. To maintain the prodigious energy required of such a project, Farrell relied on drugs: amphetamines to stay up through the night writing—he sometimes worked twenty to twenty-four hours straight, wearing the same dirty pajamas, the hotel room where he was living strewn with paper—and Valium to bring himself down, relieve his anxieties, and get some sleep.

It was, by all accounts, a frenzied and unhappy existence—until Farrell met Cleo Paturis, a magazine editor who became his partner and caretaker. She told the biographer Robert K. Landers that Farrell "needed someone to say, 'This is the time to eat breakfast,' 'This is the time to eat lunch,' . . . that kind of thing." And, with her help, Farrell stopped using drugs—at least temporarily; he later went back to taking smaller doses in secret—and settled into a normal routine. On an average day, Paturis would rise at 6:30 A.M. and fix Farrell's breakfast: orange juice, corn flakes with sliced banana, and an English muffin. While he ate, she would shower and dress, and then Farrell would walk her to the bus stop. Every time, as it drove off, he would hit the back of the bus, call out her name, and throw kisses to her, which she always returned (to the visible amusement of some of the other riders). Paturis arrived at work at 7:45, and by 8:30 she would already have her first phone call from Farrell—he called her at least six times a day. By 10:00, however, he would have started writing, and he would continue, often skipping lunch, until 5:00. Then Paturis came home, made dinner, and cleaned up the kitchen. In the evening, he answered letters while she read the newspaper.

Jackson Pollock (1912-1956)

In November 1945, Pollock and his wife and fellow painter, Lee Krasner, moved from New York to a small fishing village on eastern Long Island called Springs. Krasner had hoped that getting Pollock out of the city would stymie his drinking, and she was right: Pollock still drank, but without his bar buddies and the constant rounds of parties, he went on fewer binges and began to paint again. Indeed, the next few years in Springs were probably the happiest and most productive of his life—it was during this time that he developed the drip-painting technique for which he became famous.

Most days Pollock slept until the early afternoon. "I've got the old Eighth Street habit of sleeping all day and working all night pretty well licked," he told a visiting reporter in 1950. "So has Lee. We had to, or lose the respect of the neighbors." In fact, Krasner usually woke a few hours earlier, to clean the house, tend the garden, and perhaps work a little on her own paintings while Pollock slept—being careful to take the phone off the hook so he wouldn't be disturbed. Around 1:00 P.M., Pollock would come downstairs for his usual breakfast of coffee and cigarettes, then head out to the barn that he had converted into his studio. He would stay there until 5:00 or 6:00, then emerge for a beer and a walk to the beach with Krasner. In the evening they would have dinner and often get together with one of the area couples they had befriended (whom Krasner considered "safe company" for their benign influence on her husband). Pollock liked to stay up late, but in the country there wasn't that much to do; as he drank less he slept more, as much as twelve hours a night.

Carson McCullers (1917-1967)

McCullers's first novel was written thanks to a pact with her husband, Reeves, whom she married in 1937. The young newlyweds—Carson was twenty; Reeves twenty-four—both aspired to be writers, so they struck a deal: one of them would work full-time and earn a living for the couple while the other wrote; after a year, they would switch roles. Since McCullers already had a manuscript in progress, and Reeves had lined up a salaried position in Charlotte, North Carolina, she began her literary endeavors first.

McCullers wrote every day, sometimes escaping their drafty apartment to work in the local library, taking sips from the Thermos full of sherry that she would sneak inside. She typically worked until the middle of the afternoon, then went for a long walk. Back at the apartment, she might attempt to do some cooking or cleaning, tasks she was unused to, having grown up with servants. (McCullers later recalled trying to roast a chicken, not realizing that she had to clean the bird first. When Reeves came home, he asked her about the awful smell in the house; Carson, absorbed in her writing, hadn't even noticed.) After dinner, Carson read her day's work to Reeves, who offered his suggestions. Then the couple ate dinner, read in bed, and listened to the electric phonograph before going to sleep early.

After a year, Carson had landed a contract for her novel, so Reeves continued to put his own literary aspirations on hold and earn a salary for the both of them.

Despite the pact, he would never get to try his luck as the full-time writer in their marriage. When Carson's first novel, *The Heart Is a Lonely Hunter,* was published in 1940, it vaulted her into the literary limelight; after that, there was never any question of her sacrificing her writing for a day job and a steady paycheck.

Willem de Kooning (1904-1997)

All his life, de Kooning had a hard time getting up in the morning. He generally rose around 10:00 or 11:00, drank several strong cups of coffee, and painted all day and into the night, breaking only for dinner and the occasional visitor. When a painting was troubling him, sleep was impossible and de Kooning would spend most of the night pacing the dark streets of Manhattan. This routine changed very little after his marriage, in 1942, to Elaine Fried, a fellow artist. Mark Stevens and Annalyn Swan write:

> Typically, the couple rose late in the morning. Breakfast consisted mostly of very strong coffee, cut with the milk that they kept in winter on a window ledge; they did not have a refrigerator, an appliance that in the early forties was still a luxury. (So was a private phone, which de Kooning would not have until the early sixties.) Then the day's routine began with de Kooning moving to his end of the studio and Elaine to hers. Work was punctuated

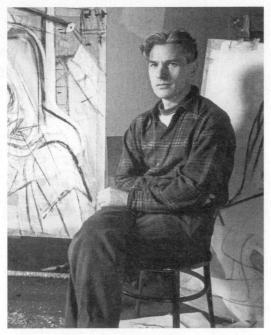

Willem de Kooning, New York, circa 1945

by more cups of strong coffee, which de Kooning
made by boiling the coffee as he had learned to
do in Holland, and by many cigarettes. The two
stayed at their easels until fairly late, taking a break
only to go out for something to eat or to walk up
to Times Square to see a movie. Often, however,
de Kooning, who hated to stop working, began
again after supper and pushed far into the night,
leaving Elaine to go to a party or concert. "I remember very often walking by and seeing the lights on

and going up," said Marjorie Luyckx. "In those studios, the heat used to go off after five o'clock because they were commercial buildings. Bill would be painting with his hat and coat on. Painting away, and whistling."

Jean Stafford (1915-1979)

A few days after learning that she had won the Pulitzer Prize for her *Collected Stories* in 1970, Stafford received a reporter from the *New York Post* in her small farmhouse on the East End of Long Island, where she had lived alone since her third husband's death seven years earlier. Looking "worn, patient, a little sad," Stafford gave the reporter a tour of the meticulously organized premises—"I'm a compulsive housekeeper," she said; "I even go into the corners with Q-tips"—and talked a little about her work habits.

Stafford wrote in her upstairs study each day, she said, from about 11:00 A.M. to 3:00 P.M. ("Does she write hard or easy?" the reporter wondered. "Hard!" Stafford replied.) The rest of the day she spent reading or pursuing a range of mild domestic hobbies: gardening, doing needlepoint, assembling potpourris, observing her two cats. Once a week she had guests over for dinner—her specialties were striped-bass chowder and barbecued spare ribs with white beans. Otherwise, she ate little, sometimes just coffee for breakfast and a Hershey bar for lunch.

At night Stafford battled with insomnia—made worse by her growing alcoholism, although she understandably did not tell the *Post* about this. Despite her drinking, the mid-1970s were some of Stafford's most productive writing years; between 1973 and 1975 she published nineteen magazine articles and reviewed a steady stream of books for several periodicals. Yet even as her work enjoyed heightened public exposure, Stafford herself became increasingly withdrawn and reclusive. She eventually called off her weekly dinner parties and began refusing visitors altogether. During the summer tourist season, she wrote in one essay, "I stay in the house with the doors locked and the blinds drawn, snarling."

Donald Barthelme (1931-1989)

While writing the stories for his first collection, *Come Back, Dr. Caligari,* Barthelme lived in Houston with his second wife, Helen, in a one-story house with a screened-in porch that he used as his office. Soon after moving into the house, in 1960, Barthelme left his job as the editor of a university literary journal to concentrate on his fiction full-time; the couple lived on Helen's two salaries, from teaching and running a small advertising business out of the house. On the first day of Barthelme's new writing career, they established a schedule that they adhered to seven days a week, and that he would largely stick to for the rest of his life.

Barthelme spent mornings on the porch, sitting down at his manual Remington typewriter at 8:00 or 9:00 and working there until noon or 1:00, the sound of his typing carrying out into the quiet neighborhood streets. For the task, he always dressed carefully in khaki or corduroy slacks, a button-down shirt, and, in cool weather, a dark gray pullover sweater. At 8:30 or 9:00, Helen brought out his breakfast of bacon or ham with toast and juice (Barthelme disliked eggs) and went to her advertising work in the dining room. Sometimes Barthelme would call to her with a question about the spelling or connotation of a particular word; and, several times each morning, he would bring her a freshly typed passage or read aloud from a new story for her feedback.

Barthelme smoked constantly while he wrote and, fearful of starting a fire, ended each session by carefully emptying his ashtray in the kitchen. He was similarly meticulous at the typewriter, reading each new sentence or phrase aloud to himself. If something didn't sound right, he would pull out the entire page, toss it in the wastebasket, and start over with a fresh sheet of newsprint. (By the end of each morning, the wastebasket would be brimming with thirty to forty discarded pages.) When he got stuck, Barthelme would head out for a twenty- or thirty-minute walk in the neighborhood. He tried not to rush the writing. Some days he would end up with one or two complete pages; other days, just a sentence or even nothing at all. For Barthelme, Helen later wrote, "the process of creativity began with dissatisfaction"; yet she also recalled, "during these first years of writing, he was irresistibly happy."

Alice Munro (b. 1931)

In the 1950s, as a young mother taking care of two small children, Munro wrote in the slivers of time she could find between housekeeping and child-rearing duties. She would often slip away to her bedroom to write in the afternoons, while her elder daughter was at school and the younger one was taking a nap. (Munro has said that she was "very big on naps" in those years.) But balancing this double life was not easy. When neighbors or acquaintances dropped in and interrupted her writing, Munro didn't feel comfortable telling them that she was trying to work; her fiction was kept secret from all but her family and closest friends. At the beginning of the 1960s, with both children in school, Munro tried renting an office above a drugstore to write a novel but gave it up after four months; even there, the garrulous landlord interrupted her and she hardly got any writing done. While Munro published short stories steadily throughout these years, it ultimately took her almost two decades to put together the material for her first collection, *Dance of the Happy Shades*, published in 1968, when she was thirty-seven years old.

Jerzy Kosinski (1933–1991)

"When he was a schoolboy, George Levanter had learned a convenient routine: a four-hour sleep in the afternoon enabled him to remain mentally and physically active until the early dawn, when he would again go to sleep for four hours and wake ready for the day." This is the first sentence of Kosinski's 1977 novel, *Blind Date,* and what the Polish-American author wrote of his protagonist was apparently true of himself, as well. In 1972, an interviewer asked Kosinski if he was "Protestant and disciplined, or European and dissolute" in his writing habits. "I guess both," Kosinski replied.

> I still wake up around 8 A.M. ready for the day, and sleep again for four hours in the afternoon, which allows me to remain mentally and physically active until the early dawn, when again I go to sleep. Being part of the Protestant ethos for less than one-third of my life, I acquired only some Protestant habits, while maintaining some of my former ones. Among the ones I acquired is the belief that I ought to answer my mail—a belief not shared by many happy intellectuals in Rome. In terms of my actual writing habits, I am an old member of the Russian and Polish intelligentsia—neither a professional intellectual nor a café-society hedonist. I love writing more than anything else. Like the heartbeat, each novel I write is inseparable from my life. I write when I feel like it and wherever I feel like it, and I feel like it most of the time: day, night, and during twilight. I write in a restaurant, on a plane, between skiing and horseback riding, when I take my night walks in Manhattan, Paris, or in any other town. I wake up in the middle of the night or the afternoon to make notes and never know when I'll sit down at the typewriter.

Isaac Asimov (1920-1992)

"The overriding factor in my life between the ages of six and twenty-two was my father's candy store," Asimov wrote in his posthumously published memoir. His father owned a succession of candy stores in Brooklyn, which he opened at 6:00 A.M. and closed at 1:00 A.M., seven days a week. Meanwhile, Young Asimov woke at 6:00 to deliver the newspaper, and rushed home from school in the afternoons to help at the store. He wrote:

> I must have liked the long hours, for in later life I never took the attitude of "I've worked hard all my childhood and youth and now I'm going to take it easy and sleep till noon."
>
> Quite the contrary. I have kept the candy-store hours all my life. I wake at five in the morning. I get to work as early as I can. I work as long as I can. I do this every day in the week, including holidays. I don't take vacations voluntarily and I try to do my work even when I'm on vacation. (And even when I'm in the hospital.)
>
> In other words, I am still and forever in the candy store. Of course, I'm not waiting on customers; I'm not taking money and making change; I'm not forced to be polite to everyone who comes in (in actual fact, I was never very good at that). I am, instead, doing things I very much want to do—but the schedule is there; the schedule that was ground into me; the schedule you would think I would have rebelled against once I had the chance.

I can only say that there were certain advantages offered by the candy store that had nothing to do with mere survival, but, rather, with overflowing happiness, and that this was so associated with the long hours as to make them sweet to me and to fix them upon me for all my life.

Oliver Sacks (b. 1933)

Sacks is a London-born, New York–based physician, professor of neurology and psychiatry, and bestselling writer, whose books include *Awakenings, The Man Who Mistook His Wife for a Hat, Musicophilia,* and *Hallucinations.*

I get up around 5 A.M. or so—not out of virtue, but because this is the way my sleep-wake cycle goes. Twice a week, I visit my analyst at 6 A.M., as I have been doing for forty years. Then I go for a swim. Swimming gets me going as nothing else can, and I need to do it at the start of the day, otherwise I will be deflected by busyness or laziness. I come back hungry from my swim, and have a large bowl of oatmeal and the first of many cups of tea, hot chocolate, or coffee which get me through the day. I use an electric kettle, in case I get preoccupied with writing and forget to turn it off.

Getting to the office—a two-minute commute, because my office and my apartment are in adjacent buildings—I look through the mail (hugely abundant now, especially with e-mail) and answer what seems to need an answer. (I do not use a computer, so I write or type my own letters.) I then have patients to see, sometimes, and writing to do, at all times. I may sketch out thoughts on my typewriter, but I generally prefer pen and paper, a Waterman fountain pen and long yellow paper. I often write at a standing desk, sometimes perched on a stool, to spare my bad back from too much sitting.

I take a brief lunch break, walk around the block, practice piano for a few minutes, and then have my favorite noon meal of herrings and black bread. The afternoon is spent writing, if I am up to it. I sometimes fall asleep, or into a deep reverie, lying on my couch, and this may put my brain in an "idling" or "default" mode. I let it play with images and thoughts on its own; I come to from these altered states, if I am lucky, with energy renewed and confused thoughts clarified.

I have an early dinner, usually tabouli and sardines (or if I have company, sushi), and play music (usually Bach) on the piano or a CD. Then I settle down to "pleasure" reading—biographies, histories, letters, occasionally novels. I hate television, and rarely watch it. I go to bed early, and usually have vivid dreams, which may haunt me until I reconstruct and (if possible) deconstruct them. I keep a notebook by my bed for memories of dreams, or night thoughts—many unexpected thoughts seem to come in the middle of the night. On the (rare) occasions when I get into a really creative mode, my daily structure is completely ignored, and I write non-stop, sometimes for 36 hours at a time, until the burst of inspiration has completed itself.

Anne Rice (b. 1941)

"I certainly have a routine, but the most important thing, when I look back over my career, has been the ability to change routines," Rice said recently. For her first novel, *Interview with the Vampire*, Rice wrote all night and slept during the day. "I just found it the time when I could concentrate and think the best," she says. "I needed to be alone in the still of the night, without the phone, without friends calling, with my husband sound asleep. I needed that utter freedom." But when her son was born in 1978, Rice made "the big switch" to daytime writing and has continued to work that way for most of her career. A few times she has switched back to a nocturnal schedule for particular novels, to get away from distractions, but she finds it too hard physically to keep up permanently.

These days she begins work in the late morning, after some time reading the newspaper, checking Facebook, and answering e-mails. She keeps writing into the afternoon, taking breaks to stretch her legs, look out the window, and drink a "massive amount" of Diet Coke on ice. In the evening she generally watches TV or a movie to relax. "That works best for me right now," she says. "But there were many times when I couldn't write until evening. And that has worked fine too. It's always a search for the uninterrupted three- or four-hour stretch."

Rice adds that for her it's "not a matter of being strict"—when beginning a new book, she tends to slip into a routine naturally, without any conscious planning. And once she's adopted a writing schedule, she doesn't need to force herself to work. But she does have to be strict about avoiding social engagements and other outside entanglements. "Because you won't get those four hours if you're spending most of the day worried about getting to an appointment and back," she says. "What you have to do is clear all distraction. That's the bottom line."

Charles Schulz (1922-2000)

Over nearly fifty years, Schulz drew every one of his 17,897 *Peanuts* comic strips by himself, without the aid of assistants. The demands of producing six daily strips and a Sunday page required a regular schedule, and Schulz fulfilled his duties in a businesslike manner, devoting seven hours a day, five days a week, to *Peanuts*. On weekdays he rose at daybreak, took a shower, shaved, and woke his children for breakfast (usually pancakes, prepared by his wife). At 8:20, Schulz drove the kids to school in the family station wagon, stopping to pick up the neighbor's children on the way. Then it was time to sit down at the drawing board, in the private studio beside his house. He would begin by doodling in pencil while he let his mind wander; his usual method was to "just sit there and think about the past, kind of dredge up ugly memories and things like that." Once he had a good idea, however, he would work quickly and with intense concentration to get it onto paper before the inspiration dried up.

Schulz stayed in his studio for lunch—almost always a ham sandwich and a glass of milk—and continued working until around 4:00, when the kids returned home from school. The regularity of the work suited his temperament and helped him cope with the chronic anxiety he suffered throughout his life. "I would feel just terrible if I couldn't draw comic strips," Schulz once said. "I would feel very empty if I were not allowed to do this sort of thing."

William Gass (b. 1924)

Gass is an early riser. In a 1998 interview, he said that he works mostly in the morning, finishing his serious writing by noon. Afternoons are spent on his academic duties—in addition to writing fiction, he has taught philosophy for most of his career—and "other kinds of work which is more mechanical." A colleague once asked Gass if he had any unusual writing habits:

> "No, sorry to be boring," he sighed. . . . "How does your day begin?" "Oh, I go out and photograph for a couple of hours," he said. "What do you photograph?" "The rusty, derelict, overlooked, downtrodden parts of the city. Filth and decay mainly," he said in a nothing-much-to-it tone of voice, as

casually dismissive as the wave of a hand. "You do this every day, photograph filth and decay?" "Most days." "And then you write?" "Yes." "And you don't think that's unusual?" "Not for me."

Gass has also said that he writes best when he's angry, which can take a toll on his health over the course of long writing projects. (It took him twenty-five years to complete his 1995 novel, *The Tunnel*.) "I get very tense working, so I often have to get up and wander around the house," he said in 1976. "It is very bad on my stomach. I have to be mad to be working well anyway, and then I am mad about the way things are going on the page in addition. My ulcer flourishes and I have to chew lots of pills. When my work is going well, I am usually sort of sick."

David Foster Wallace (1962-2008)

"I usually go in shifts of three or four hours with either naps or, like, you know, fairly diverting do-something-with-other-people things in the middle," Wallace said in 1996, shortly after the publication of *Infinite Jest*. "So, like, I'll get up at eleven or noon, work till two or three." In later interviews, however, Wallace said that he followed a regular writing routine only when the work was going badly. From a 1999 radio interview:

Things are either going well or they're not going well. . . . I'm working on something now and I just can't seem to get it. I flounder and I flounder.

And when I'm floundering I don't want to work, so I invent draconian "All right, this morning I'll work from seven-thirty to eight-forty-five with one five-minute break"—all this baroque b.s. And after five or ten or a dozen or, you know, as with some books, fifty tries, all of a sudden it will just, it will start to go. And once it starts to go, it requires no effort. And then actually the discipline's required in terms of being willing to be away from it and to remember that, "Oh, I have a relationship that I have to nurture or I have to grocery shop or pay these bills" and stuff. So I have absolutely no routine at all, because the times I'm trying to build a routine are the times that the writing just seems futile and flagellating.

Marina Abramović (b. 1946)

In her four-decade career as a performance artist, Abramović has forced herself into displays of tremendous (and often shocking) discipline and endurance. For her 2010 career retrospective at the Museum of Modern Art, in New York, Abramović staged a particularly grueling piece. Called *The Artist Is Present,* it required her to sit motionless in a chair every hour that the exhibition was open—seven hours a day (ten hours on Fridays), six days a week, for eleven weeks. Each day, museum visitors were invited to sit in a chair opposite her for as long as they liked; by the end of the eleven weeks, Abramović had gazed at 1,565 pairs of eyes. To prepare for the performance, she had to train her body to go all day without food and without urinating. (There was some speculation in the press that she was wearing a catheter or a diaper, but Abramović insists that she just held it in.)

She began building a routine three months before the opening. Her biggest challenge was to go all day without taking any fluids. To get the water her body needed, Abramović adopted a nocturnal hydration regimen. Throughout the night, she forced herself to get up every forty-five minutes to drink a small amount of water. "At the beginning I was exhausted," she says. "And then at the end I kind of trained myself and actually I could drink the water without interrupting my sleep in a certain way."

On performance days, Abramović would wake up at 6:30 A.M., take a bath, and at 7:00 have her last drink of water for the day. Then she would eat a meal of lentils and rice and drink a cup of black tea. At 9:00 a car would take Abramović, her assistant, and her photographer to MoMA, and Abramović would change into her dress. Over the next forty-five minutes she would visit the bathroom four times, emptying her bladder completely. Then she would draw a line on the wall to mark the previous day's completed performance and sit by herself for fifteen minutes before visitors began to arrive.

Seven or ten hours later, Abramović would return home, eat a light vegetarian meal, and be in bed by 10:00 P.M., continuing to take a small amount of water every forty-five minutes through the night. At no point in the day did she talk on the phone or answer e-mails. "I completely cut communications," she says. "I didn't talk except with the guard at the museum, the curator, and my assistant and photographer. No phone calls, no talking, no meetings, no interviews. Nothing. Everything stopped."

This is typical of Abramović's working style. When she has a new idea for a performance, it takes over her life. But when she is not giving a performance or preparing for one, she is a different creature entirely. "In my personal life, if I don't have a project, I don't have any discipline," she says. Neither does she follow a regular daily routine. "I don't have any particular everyday kind of thing," she says. "Only when I know that I have to do the performance, then I absolutely concentrate on that in a rigorous way."

Twyla Tharp (b. 1941)

Tharp is something of an expert on daily routines. The choreographer's 2003 book, *The Creative Habit,* is all about the necessity of forming good, consistent work habits in order to function at a high creative level. Not surprisingly, her own routine is intense:

> I begin each day of my life with a ritual: I wake up at 5:30 A.M., put on my workout clothes, my leg warmers, my sweatshirts, and my hat. I walk outside my Manhattan home, hail a taxi, and tell the driver to take me to the Pumping Iron gym at 91st Street and First Avenue, where I work out for two hours. The ritual is not the stretching and weight training I put

my body through each morning at the gym; the ritual is the cab. The moment I tell the driver where to go I have completed the ritual.

By automatically getting up and getting into the cab every morning, she avoids the question of whether or not she feels like going to the gym; the ritual is one less thing for her to think about, as well as "a friendly reminder that I'm doing the right thing." But the 5:30 cab is only one item in her "arsenal of routines." As she writes later in the book:

I repeat the wake-up, the workout, the quick shower, the breakfast of three hard-boiled egg whites and a cup of coffee, the hour to make my morning calls and deal with correspondence, the two hours of stretching and working out ideas by myself in the studio, the rehearsals with my dance company, the return home in the late afternoon to handle more business details, the early dinner, and a few quiet hours of reading. That's my day, every day. A dancer's life is all about repetition.

Tharp admits that this schedule does not allow for a particularly sociable life. "It's actively anti-social," she writes. "On the other hand, it is pro-creative." And, for her, that daily creativity is sustaining: "When it all comes together, a creative life has the nourishing power we normally associate with food, love, and faith."

Stephen King (b. 1947)

King writes every day of the year, including his birthday and holidays, and he almost never lets himself quit before he reaches his daily quota of two thousand words. He works in the mornings, starting around 8:00 or 8:30. Some days he finishes up as early as 11:30, but more often it takes him until about 1:30 to meet his goal. Then he has the afternoons and evenings free for naps, letters, reading, family, and Red Sox games on TV.

In his memoir *On Writing,* King compares fiction writing to "creative sleep," and his writing routine to getting ready for bed each night:

> Like your bedroom, your writing room should be private, a place where you go to dream. Your schedule—in at about the same time every day, out when your thousand words are on paper or disk— exists in order to habituate yourself, to make yourself ready to dream just as you make yourself ready to sleep by going to bed at roughly the same time each night and following the same ritual as you go. In both writing and sleeping, we learn to be physically still at the same time we are encouraging our minds to unlock from the humdrum rational thinking of our daytime lives. And as your mind and body grow accustomed to a certain amount of sleep each night—six hours, seven, maybe the recommended eight—so can you train your waking mind to sleep creatively and work out the vividly imagined waking dreams which are successful works of fiction.

Marilynne Robinson (b. 1943)

"I really am incapable of discipline," Robinson told *The Paris Review* in 2008.

> I write when something makes a strong claim on me. When I don't feel like writing, I absolutely don't feel like writing. I tried that work ethic thing a couple of times—I can't say I exhausted its possibilities—but if there's not something on my mind that I really want to write about, I tend to write something that I hate. And that depresses me. I don't want to look at it. I don't want to live through the time it takes for it to go up the chimney. Maybe it's a question of discipline, maybe temperament, who knows?

Not surprisingly, Robinson does not stick to a particular writing schedule—but she does use her frequent sleeplessness to her advantage. "I have benevolent insomnia," she said. "I wake up, and my mind is preternaturally clear. The world is quiet. I can read or write. It seems like stolen time. It seems like I have a twenty-eight-hour day."

Saul Bellow (1915-2005)

"Someone once called me a bureaucrat (among writers) because my self-discipline seemed excessive," Bellow told an interviewer in 1964. "It seemed excessive to me too." Bellow wrote every day, beginning early in the morning and breaking off around lunchtime. In his 2000 biography, James Atlas described the novelist's working habits in the 1970s, when he was living in Chicago and writing the novel *Humboldt's Gift*:

> Rising promptly at six o'clock in the morning, he would fortify himself with two cups of strong coffee heated in a pan and get down to work. From his window, he looked out at a university playing field and, in the distance, the spires of Rockefeller Chapel. Often still in his ragged striped bathrobe when the typist arrived, he would sit down in a chair beside her and dictate from the notes he'd accumulated the night before—up to twenty pages a day. Like Dickens, who wrote his books with company in the living room, Bellow thrived on chaos. In the midst of composition, he fielded phone calls from editors and travel agents, friends and students; stood on his head to restore concentration; bantered with his son Daniel when he was staying at the house. He generally broke off at noon, did thirty push-ups, and had a simple lunch of tuna salad or smoked whitefish, accompanied—if the work had gone well—by a glass of wine or a shot of gin.

In a 1968 letter, Bellow gave a more succinct description of his routine. "I simply get up in the morning and go to work, and I read at night," he wrote. "Like Abe Lincoln."

Gerhard Richter (b. 1932)

Richter wakes at 6:15 every morning, makes breakfast for his family, and takes his daughter to school at 7:20. He's in his backyard studio by 8:00, and he stays there until 1:00. Then he eats the lunch laid out for him in the dining room by the housekeeper: yogurt, tomatoes, bread, olive oil, and chamomile tea. After lunch, he goes back to the studio and works into the evening—although he admits that it's not all focused work. "I go to the studio every day, but I don't paint every day," he told a reporter in 2002.

> I love playing with my architectural models. I love making plans. I could spend my life arranging things. Weeks go by, and I don't paint until finally I can't stand it any longer. I get fed up. I almost don't want to talk about it, because I don't want to become self-conscious about it, but perhaps I create these little crises as a kind of a secret strategy to push myself. It is a danger to wait around for an idea to occur to you. You have to find the idea.

Jonathan Franzen (b. 1959)

Shortly after graduating from college, Franzen married his girlfriend, also an aspiring novelist, and the pair settled down to work in classic starving-artist fashion. They found an apartment outside Boston for $300 a month, stocked up on ten-pound bags of rice and enormous packages of frozen chicken, and allowed themselves to eat out only once a year, on their anniversary. When their savings ran out, Franzen got a weekend job as a research assistant at Harvard University's seismology department, which paid the bills for them both. Five days a week, the couple wrote for eight hours a day, ate dinner, and then read for four or five more hours. "I was frantically driven," Franzen said. "I got up after breakfast, sat down at the desk and worked till dark, basically. One of us would work in the dining room, and the kitchen was interposed, and then the bedroom was on the other side. It was workable, for newlyweds." It wasn't workable forever. Eventually the marriage dissolved, in part due to the lopsidedness of their creative venture: as Franzen's first two books came out to positive reviews, his wife's first manuscript failed to find a publisher and her second one stalled midway.

But Franzen's subsequent literary efforts didn't come any easier. To force himself to concentrate on his 2001 novel, *The Corrections,* he would seal himself in his Harlem studio with the blinds drawn and the lights off, sitting before the computer keyboard wearing earplugs, earmuffs, and a blindfold. It still took him four years, and thousands of discarded pages, to complete the book. "I was in such a harmful pattern," he told a reporter afterward. "In a way, it would begin on a Friday, when I would realize what I'd been working on all week was bad. I would polish it all day to bring up the gloss, until by four in the afternoon I'd have to admit it was bad. Between five and six, I'd get drunk on vodka—shot glasses. Then have dinner, much too late, consumed with a sick sense of failure. I hated myself the entire time."

Maira Kalman (b. 1949)

The New York illustrator, artist, and designer wakes up early, about 6:00 A.M., makes the bed, and reads the obituaries. Then she goes for a walk with a friend, returns home to eat breakfast, and—if she's on deadline—heads to her studio, in the same building as her apartment. "I have no phone, or email, no food or anything to distract [in the studio]," she said in a recent e-mail. "I have music and work. There is a green chaise there if a nap is needed. And in the late afternoon it is often needed."

If she is bored being alone in the studio, Kalman will head to a café to listen to the buzz of conversation, take the subway to a museum, or go for a walk through Central Park. "I procrastinate just the right amount," she said. "There are things which help me get in the mood to work. Cleaning for one. Ironing is great. Taking a walk is always inspiring. Because my work is often based on what I see, I am happy to keep collecting and changing images until the last moment."

Sometimes Kalman doesn't go into the studio for days at a time. On working days, she is done by 6:00 P.M. She never works at night. "It will appear like a calm existence," Kalman said. "The turmoil is invisible."

Georges Simenon (1903-1989)

Simenon was one of the most prolific novelists of the twentieth century, publishing 425 books in his career, including more than 200 works of pulp fiction under 16 different pseudonyms, as well as 220 novels in his own name and three volumes of autobiography. Remarkably, he didn't write every day. The Belgian-French novelist worked in intense bursts of literary activity, each lasting two or three weeks, separated by weeks or months of no writing at all.

Even during his productive weeks, Simenon didn't write for very long each day. His typical schedule was to wake at 6:00 A.M., procure coffee, and write from 6:30 to 9:30. Then he would go for a long walk, eat lunch at 12:30, and take a one-hour nap. In the afternoon he spent time with his children and took another walk before dinner, television, and bed at 10:00 P.M.

Simenon liked to portray himself as a methodical writing machine—he could compose up to eighty typed pages in a session, making virtually no revisions after the

Georges Simenon steps into his home office in Paris. The "Do Not Disturb" was to be taken seriously.

fact—but he did have his share of superstitious behaviors. No one ever saw him working; the "Do Not Disturb" sign he hung on his door was to be taken seriously. He insisted on wearing the same clothes throughout the composition of each novel. He kept tranquilizers in his shirt pocket, in case he needed to ease the anxiety that beset him at the beginning of each new book. And he weighed himself before and after every book, estimating that each one cost him nearly a liter and a half of sweat.

Simenon's astonishing literary productivity was matched, or even surpassed, in one other area of his daily life—his sexual appetite. "Most people work every day and enjoy sex periodically," Patrick Marnham notes in his biography of the writer. "Simenon had sex every day and every few months indulged in a frenzied orgy of work." When living in Paris, Simenon frequently slept with four different women in the same day. He estimated that he bedded ten thousand women in his life. (His second wife disagreed, putting the total closer to twelve hundred.) He explained his sexual hunger as the result of "extreme curiosity" about the opposite sex: "Women have always been exceptional people for me whom I have vainly tried to understand. It has been a lifelong, ceaseless quest. And how could I have created dozens, perhaps hundreds, of female characters in my novels if I had not experienced those adventures which lasted for two hours or ten minutes?"

Stephen Jay Gould (1941-2002)

"I work all the time," the evolutionary biologist and writer told an interviewer in 1991.

I work every day. I work weekends, I work nights.... [S]ome people looking at that from the outside might use that modern term "workaholic," or might see this as obsessive or destructive. But it's not work to me, it's just what I do, that's my life. I also spend a lot of time with my family, and I sing, and go to ball games, and you can find me in my season seat at Fenway Park as often as—well, I don't mean I have a one-dimensional life. But I basically do work all the time. I don't watch television. But it's not work, it's not work, it's my life. It's what I do. It's what I like to do.

Asked to account for his formidable work ethic, Gould said he thinks it's ultimately a question of temperament—"some odd and inextricable mixture of lucky accidents of birth and inheritance and an encouraging environment."

You have to have high levels of bodily energy and not everybody has it. I'm not physically strong, but I have very great intellectual energy, I always have. I've been able to work all day. I don't have to get up and get a drink of water or watch TV for half an hour. I can literally sit and work all day once I get going, not everybody can do that. It's not a moral issue. Some people seem to see that as a moral question. It isn't. It's a question of body type and temperament and energy levels. I don't know what makes us what we are.

Bernard Malamud (1914-1986)

The novelist and short-story writer was, in the words of his biographer, Philip Davis, a "time-haunted man." Malamud's daughter remembers him being "absolutely, compulsively prompt" throughout his life, and notes that he could become extremely agitated when made late. This obsessive punctuality served him well as a writer. Although he made his living as a teacher for most of his life, Malamud always found time to write and apparently never lacked for discipline. "Discipline is an ideal for the self," he once said. "If you have to discipline yourself to achieve art, you discipline yourself."

Malamud began writing seriously in 1940, when he was twenty-six, and soon after landed a job teaching night school in Brooklyn. His classes were from 6:00 until 10:00 in the evening, so he was able to write for five hours during the day, typically between 10:00 A.M. and 5:00 P.M. with a break at 12:30 to eat lunch, shave, and read for an hour. After eight years of this schedule, Malamud accepted a university teaching position in Oregon, moving there in 1949 with his wife and their young son. At the time, he had yet even to sell a story. But over the next dozen years he wrote four books, thanks in part to a favorable teaching schedule. Mondays, Wednesdays, and

Fridays were devoted to classes, office hours, and grading papers; Tuesdays, Thursdays, and Saturdays Malamud spent on his novels and short stories ("and I sneak parts of Sundays," he said).

On writing days in Oregon, Malamud rose at 7:30, exercised for ten minutes, ate breakfast, and arrived at his office by 9:00. A full morning of writing usually amounted to only a page, two at best. After lunch, he revised the morning's output, then returned home around 4:00. A short nap preceded domestic activities: dinner at 6:15, conversation with the family, help with the children's homework. After the kids went to sleep, Malamud read for three hours—he usually spent half the time on fiction, half on nonfiction connected to his stories and novels—before going to sleep at midnight.

Although he was a creature of habit, Malamud was wary of placing too much importance on his particular work rituals. He told an interviewer:

> There's no one way—there's too much drivel about this subject. You're who you are, not Fitzgerald or Thomas Wolfe. You write by sitting down and writing. There's no particular time or place—you suit yourself, your nature. How one works, assuming he's disciplined, doesn't matter. If he or she is not disciplined, no sympathetic magic will help. The trick is to make time—not steal it—and produce the fiction. If the stories come, you get them written, you're on the right track. Eventually everyone learns his or her own best way. The real mystery to crack is you.

ACKNOWLEDGMENTS

My first debt is to the hundreds of writers and editors whose works I consulted for this collection; without their original scholarship, this book would have been impossible. In addition, several creative professionals took time out of their busy schedules to answer my questions about their routines and working habits (and, in the end, I was unable to include all of their contributions). I am grateful to them for their generosity.

This book may never have happened without my agent, Megan Thompson, who e-mailed me out of the blue, convinced me that my *Daily Routines* blog could be a successful book, and found a perfect home for it at Knopf. Her colleagues Sandy Hodgman and Molly Reese have been extremely helpful along the way. I would also like to thank Laurence Kirshbaum for his support.

At Knopf, I was fortunate to have Victoria Wilson as my editor. She gave me the freedom to do this book exactly as I wanted to but then did not let it move forward until it met her high standards. The results are greatly improved by her good judgment. Her colleagues Carmen Johnson and Daniel Schwartz took care of countless details with unflagging patience and aplomb. Many thanks to the jacket designer, Jason Booher; the text designer, Maggie Hinders; and the production editor, Victoria Pearson.

I owe a special debt of gratitude to Martin Pedersen, who helped me hang on to my day job and did me the great kindness of constantly asking how the book was coming along. Belinda Lanks, James Ryerson, and Michael Silverberg were among the first people to see the *Daily Routines* blog, and their enthusiasm and suggestions were vital to its success. Many readers of the blog also wrote with leads, some of which proved invaluable; I was lucky to have such an intelligent and engaged audience. Lindy Hess gave me advice on the publishing business. Stephen Kozlowski lent his superior eye for the author photo.

All of my friends and family have been incredibly encouraging during this long process. I would particularly like to thank my mom; my dad; my stepmom, Barbee; and my brother, Andrew, for their total, unwavering support. Finally, my own daily routine would be very dull without my wife, Rebecca, who is a constant source of joy and inspiration.

NOTES

For each entry in the book, I have provided reference information for my source or sources, keyed to the subject's name. When there are multiple sources, I have listed them in approximate order of their importance—that is, in how much I relied upon them for the entry. After that, I have also provided the exact location of all quotes and a number of specific details and assertions. I hope that this will make it easy for readers to find more information on particular subjects' routines, habits, quirks, and foibles.

vii   **"Who can unravel"**: Thomas Mann, *Death in Venice*, trans. Michael Henry Heim (New York: Ecco, 2005), 88.

viii   **"Tell me what"**: Jean Anthelme Brillat-Savarin, *The Physiology of Taste: Or, Meditations on Transcendental Gastronomy*, trans. M. F. K. Fisher (1949; repr. Washington, D.C.: Counterpoint, 1999), 3.

xiv   **"free our minds"**: Quoted in Robert D. Richardson, *William James: In the Maelstrom of American Modernism* (Boston: Houghton Mifflin, 2006), 121.

xvi   **"Sooner or later"**: V. S. Pritchett, "Gibbon and the Home Guard," in *Complete Collected Essays* (New York: Random House, 1991), 4.

xvii   **"time is short"**: Franz Kafka to Felice Bauer, November 1, 1912, in *Letters to Felice*, ed. Erich Heller and Jürgen Born, trans. James Stern and Elisabeth Duckworth (New York: Schocken Books, 1973), 21–2.

3   **W. H. Auden**: Humphrey Carpenter, *W. H. Auden: A Biography* (Boston: Houghton Mifflin, 1981); Richard

Davenport-Hines, *Auden* (New York: Pantheon Books, 1995); Stephen Spender, ed., *W. H. Auden: A Tribute* (New York: Macmillan, 1975).

3 "Routine, in an": Quoted in Davenport-Hines, 298.

3 "He checks his": Quoted in Carpenter, 391.

3 "A modern stoic": Quoted in Davenport-Hines, 298.

3 "Only the 'Hitlers'": Quoted in Spender, 173.

4 "the chemical life": Quoted in Carpenter, 265.

4 "labor-saving devices": Quoted in Davenport-Hines, 186.

4 Francis Bacon: Michael Peppiatt, *Francis Bacon: Anatomy of an Enigma* (New York: Farrar, Straus and Giroux, 1996).

5 "essentially a creature": Ibid., 101.

6 "I often like": Quoted ibid., 161.

6 Simone de Beauvoir: Interview with Bernard Frechtman and Madeleine Gobeil, "The Art of Fiction No. 35: Simone de Beauvoir," *Paris Review*, Spring–Summer 1965, http://www.theparisreview.org/interviews/4444/the-art-of-fiction-no-35-simone-de-beauvoir; Deirdre Bair, *Simone de Beauvoir: A Biography* (New York: Touchstone, 1990); Louis Menand, "Stand By Your Man," *New Yorker*, September 26, 2005, http://www.newyorker.com/archive/2005/09/26/050926crbo_books.

6 "I'm always in": Interview with Frechtman and Gobeil.

7 Generally, Beauvoir worked: Bair, 359–60.

8 "On the first": Quoted ibid., 444.

9 Thomas Wolfe: David Herbert Donald, *Look Homeward: A Life of Thomas Wolfe* (Boston: Little, Brown, 1987).

9 "amazing speed": Quoted ibid., 237.

9 "penis remained limp": Quoted ibid.

9 "male configurations": Quoted ibid.

9 "priming himself with": Ibid., 246.

10 Patricia Highsmith: Andrew Wilson, *Beautiful Shadow: A Life of Patricia Highsmith* (London: Bloomsbury, 2003).

10 "There is no": Quoted ibid., 324.

10 like rats have: Ibid., 8.

10 "Her favourite technique": Ibid., 123.

11 "not to perk": Ibid., 141.

11 "she only ever": Quoted ibid., 323.

12 "they give me": Quoted ibid., 135.

12 Federico Fellini: Hollis Alpert, *Fellini: A Life* (1986; repr.

New York: Paragon House, 1988); Bert Cardullo, ed., *Federico Fellini: Interviews* (Jackson: University Press of Mississippi, 2006).

12 **"I'm up at six"**: Quoted in Alpert, 264.

13 **"A writer can"**: Interview with Gideon Bachmann, *Film Book I*, ed. Robert Hughes (New York: Grove, 1959), in Cardullo, 16.

13 **Ingmar Bergman**: Raphael Shargel, ed., *Ingmar Bergman: Interviews* (Jackson: University Press of Mississippi, 2007); Michiko Kakutani, "Ingmar Bergman: Summing Up a Life in Film," *New York Times Magazine*, June 6, 1983, http://www.nytimes.com/1983/06/06/magazine/26kaku.html.

13 **"Do you know"**: Interview with Cynthia Grenier, *Playboy*, June 1964, in Shargel, 38.

13 **"He constantly eats"**: Interview with Richard Meryman, "I Live at the Edge of a Very Strange Country," *Life*, October 15, 1971, in Shargel, 107.

14 **"I never use"**: Ibid., 103.

14 **"I have been"**: Quoted in Kakutani.

14 **Morton Feldman**: Chris Villars, ed. and trans., *Morton Feldman Says: Selected Interviews and Lectures 1964–1987* (London: Hyphen, 2006); B. H. Friedman, ed., *Give My Regards to Eighth Street: Collected Writings of Morton Feldman* (Cambridge, MA: Exact Change, 2000).

14 **"I live here"**: Interview with Martine Cadieu in Villars, 39.

15 **"the most important"**: Morton Feldman, "Darmstadt Lecture," July 26, 1984, in Villars, 204.

15 **"My concern at times"**: Morton Feldman, "The Anxiety of Art," *Art in America*, September/October 1973, in Friedman, 30.

16 **Wolfgang Amadeus Mozart**: Emily Anderson, trans. and ed., *The Letters of Mozart and His Family*, 3rd ed. (New York: W. W. Norton, 1985); Peter Gay, *Mozart* (New York: Viking Penguin, 1999).

16 **"My hair is always"**: Mozart to his sister, February 17, 1782, in Anderson, 797.

17 **"Altogether I have"**: Mozart to his father, December 28, 1782, in Anderson, 833.

17 **"It is impossible"**: Leopold Mozart to his daughter, March 12, 1785, in Anderson, 888.

17 **Ludwig van Beethoven:** Anton Felix Schindler, *Beethoven As I Knew Him,* ed. Donald W. MacArdle, trans. Constance S. Jolly (1860; repr. Mineola, NY: Dover, 1996); Maynard Solomon, *Beethoven,* 2nd rev. ed. (New York: Schirmer Books, 1998).

18 **"Washing and bathing":** Schindler, 386.

19 **Søren Kierkegaard:** Joakim Garff, *Søren Kierkegaard: A Biography,* trans. Bruce H. Kirmmse (Princeton, NJ: Princeton University Press, 2005).

19 **"at least fifty":** Quoted ibid., 290.

20 **"Kierkegaard had":** Ibid., 291.

20 **Voltaire:** Roger Pearson, *Voltaire Almighty: A Life in Pursuit of Freedom* (New York and London: Bloomsbury, 2005); Haydn Mason, *Voltaire: A Biography* (Baltimore: Johns Hopkins University Press, 1981).

20 **recorded Voltaire's routine:** Pearson, 355.

21 **Wagnière estimated that:** Mason, 134.

21 **"I love the cell":** Quoted ibid.

21 **Benjamin Franklin:** Benjamin Franklin, *The Autobiography and Other Writings,* ed. Peter Shaw (New York: Bantam Books, 1982); H. W. Brands, *The First American: The Life and Times of Benjamin Franklin,* 2nd ed. (New York: Anchor Books, 2002).

21 **"moral perfection":** Franklin, 75.

21 **"Let all your things":** Ibid., 76.

23 **"I have found it":** Quoted in Brands, 411.

23 **Anthony Trollope:** Anthony Trollope, *An Autobiography* (1883; repr. New York: Dodd, Mead and Company, 1922); Pamela Neville-Sington, *Fanny Trollope: The Life and Adventures of a Clever Woman* (New York: Viking, 1997).

24 **"It was my practice":** Trollope, 236–7.

25 **mother, Francis Trollope:** Neville-Sington, 255.

25 **Jane Austen:** Park Honan, *Jane Austen: Her Life* (New York: Fawcett Columbine, 1987); James Edward Austen-Leigh, *Memoir of Jane Austen* (1926; repr. Oxford: Oxford University Press, 1967); Carol Shields, *Jane Austen* (New York: Viking Penguin, 2001).

26 **"subject to all":** Austen-Leigh, 102.

26 **Austen rose early:** Honan, 264.

27 **"Composition seems to":** Quoted in Shields, 123.

27 **Frédéric Chopin:** Jim Samson, *Chopin* (New York: Schirmer Books, 1996); Frederick Niecks, *Frederick Chopin As a Man and Musician*, vol. 2 (1888; repr. Neptune City, NJ: Paganiniana, 1980).

27 **"His creation was":** Quoted in Niecks, 132.

29 **"I dared not":** Ibid.

29 **Gustave Flaubert:** Francis Steegmuller, *Flaubert and Madame Bovary: A Double Portrait* (1939; repr. New York: New York Review of Books, 2005); Frederick Brown, *Flaubert: A Biography* (New York: Little, Brown, 2006); Henry Troyat, *Flaubert*, trans. Joan Pinkham (New York: Viking, 1992).

29 **already looking middle-aged:** Steegmuller, 216.

30 **"Last night I began":** Quoted in Troyat, 111.

30 **Flaubert woke at 10:00:** Brown, 293, and Steegmuller, 239–41.

31 **"Sometimes I don't":** Quoted in Troyat, 117.

32 **"*Bovary* is not":** Quoted ibid., 126.

32 **Together they would:** Steegmuller, 241.

32 **"After all":** Quoted in Troyat, 173.

33 **Henri de Toulouse-Lautrec:** Julia Frey, *Toulouse-Lautrec: A Life* (New York: Viking, 1994); Jad Adams, *Hideous Absinthe: A History of the Devil in a Bottle* (London: I. B. Tauris, 2004).

34 **One of his inventions:** Adams, 132.

34 **"a peacock's tail":** Quoted ibid.

34 **"I expect to burn":** Quoted in Frey, 242.

34 **Thomas Mann:** Anthony Heilbut, *Thomas Mann: Eros and Literature* (1995; repr. Berkeley and Los Angeles: University of California Press, 1997); Ronald Hayman, *Thomas Mann: A Biography* (New York: Scribner, 1995).

34 **"Every passage becomes":** Quoted in Heilbut, 207.

35 **"clench the teeth":** Quoted ibid.

36 **Karl Marx:** Isaiah Berlin, *Karl Marx: His Life and Environment*, 4th ed. (New York: Oxford University Press, 1996); Francis Wheen, *Karl Marx: A Life* (New York: W. W. Norton, 2000); Michael Evans, *Karl Marx* (Bloomington and London: Indiana University Press, 1975); Werner Blumenberg, *Karl Marx: An Illustrated Biography*, trans. Douglas Scott (1972; repr. London: Verso, 1998).

36 "His mode of living": Berlin, 143.

37 He never had: Evans, 32.

37 "I must pursue": Quoted ibid.

37 Marx relied on: Wheen, 160.

37 "I don't suppose": Quoted ibid., 234.

37 "could neither sit": Blumenberg, 100.

37 "You know that": Quoted in Evans, 33.

38 Sigmund Freud: Peter Gay, *Freud: A Life for Our Time* (1988; repr. New York: W. W. Norton, 1998); Martin Freud, *Sigmund Freud: Man and Father* (New York: Vanguard Press, 1958); Louis Breger, *Freud: Darkness in the Midst of Vision* (New York: Wiley, 2000).

38 "I cannot imagine": Quoted in Gay, 157.

38 "My father marched": Freud, 27.

39 "My boy, smoking": Quoted in Gay, 170.

39 Carl Jung: Ronald Hayman, *A Life of Jung* (1999; repr. New York: W. W. Norton, 2001); Carl Jung, *Memories, Dreams, Reflections*, ed. Aniela Jaffé, trans. Richard and Clara Winston, rev. ed. (1961; repr. New York: Vintage Books, 1989).

40 "If a man": Quoted in Hayman, 250.

41 "I've realized that": Quoted ibid., 310.

41 "spent a long time": Ibid., 251.

41 "At Bollingen I": Jung, 225-6.

41 Gustav Mahler: Alma Mahler, *Gustav Mahler: Memories and Letters*, ed. Donald Mitchell, trans. Basil Creighton (1946; repr. New York: Viking Press, 1969); Henry-Louis De La Grange, *Gustav Mahler*, vol. 2 (Oxford: Oxford University Press, 1995).

42 "was stripped of": Mahler, 47.

42 "he nearly always": Ibid., 45.

43 "Its purpose was": Ibid., 46.

43 "an invalid's diet": Ibid.

44 "If his inspiration": Ibid., 47.

44 "There's such a": Quoted in De La Grange, 536.

44 "You know that": Quoted ibid., 534.

44 Richard Strauss: Norman Del Mar, *Richard Strauss: A Critical Commentary on His Life and Works*, vol. 1 (1962; repr. London: Barrie and Jenkins, 1978).

45 "My day's work": Quoted ibid., 91.

45 Henri Matisse: Interview with Francis Carco, "Conversa-

tions with Matisse," *Die Kunst-Zeitung*, August 8, 1943, trans. and repr. in *Matisse on Art,* Jack D. Flam (1973; repr. New York: E. P. Dutton, 1978), 82–90.

45 **"Basically, I enjoy"**: Quoted ibid., 85.

46 **"Do you understand"**: Quoted ibid.

47 **Joan Miró**: Lluis Permanyer, *Miró: The Life of a Passion,* trans. Paul Martin (Barcelona: Edicions de 1984, 2003).

47 **"[A]t six o'clock"**: Ibid., 105.

49 **"Merde! I absolutely"**: Quoted ibid., 107.

49 **Gertrude Stein**: Janet Flanner, James Thurber, and Harold Ross, "Tender Buttons," The Talk of the Town, *New Yorker,* October, 13, 1934, http://www.newyorker.com/archive/1934 /10/13/1934_10_13_022_TNY_CARDS_000238137; Gertrude Stein, *Everybody's Autobiography* (1937; repr. Cambridge, MA: Exact Change, 1993); Janet Malcolm, *Two Lives: Gertrude and Alice* (New Haven, CT: Yale University Press, 2007).

49 **"managed the practical"**: Malcolm., 28.

49 **"Miss Stein gets up"**: Flanner et al.

51 **"If you write"**: Stein, 70.

51 **"I never go"**: Ibid., 134.

51 **Ernest Hemingway**: Interview with George Plimpton, "The Art of Fiction No. 21: Ernest Hemingway," *Paris Review,* 1958, http://www.theparisreview.org/interviews/4825/the -art-of-fiction-no-21-ernest-hemingway; Gregory H. Hemingway, M.D., *Papa: A Personal Memoir* (Boston: Houghton Mifflin, 1976).

51 **"My father would"**: Hemingway, 49.

52 **"When I am"**: Interview with Plimpton.

52 **"I don't think"**: Ibid.

52 **"so as not to"**: Ibid.

53 **"the awful responsibility"**: Quoted in Hemingway, 49.

53 **Henry Miller**: Frank L. Kersnowski and Alice Hughes, eds., *Conversations with Henry Miller* (Jackson: University Press of Mississippi, 1994).

53 **"I don't believe"**: Quoted in Audrey June Booth, "An Interview with Henry Miller," 1962, in ibid., 41–2.

53 **"I know that"**: Quoted in Lionel Olay, "Meeting with Henry," *Cavalier,* July 1963, in Kersnowski and Hughes, 70.

53 **F. Scott Fitzgerald**: Matthew J. Bruccoli, *Some Sort of*

Epic Grandeur: The Life of F. Scott Fitzgerald, 2nd rev. ed. (Columbia: University of South Carolina Press, 2002); Jeffrey Meyers, *Scott Fitzgerald: A Biography* (New York: HarperCollins, 1994).

54 **"Stories are best"**: Quoted in Bruccoli, 109.

55 **"It has become"**: Quoted ibid., 341.

55 **William Faulkner:** Jay Parini, *One Matchless Time: A Life of William Faulkner* (New York: HarperCollins, 2004); Stephen B. Oates, *William Faulkner: The Man and the Artist* (New York: Harper and Row, 1987); David Minter, *William Faulkner: His Life and Work* (Baltimore: Johns Hopkins University Press, 1980).

56 **"always wrote when"**: Quoted in Parini, 217.

56 **"I write when"**: Quoted in Oates, 96.

56 **Arthur Miller:** Interview with Christopher Bigby, "The Art of Theater No. 2, Part 2: Arthur Miller," *Paris Review,* Fall 1999, http://www.theparisreview.org/interviews/895/the-art -of-theater-no-2-part-2-arthur-miller.

57 **Benjamin Britten:** Christopher Headington, *Britten* (London: Omnibus Press, 1996); Alan Blyth, *Remembering Britten* (London: Hutchinson, 1981).

57 **"That isn't the way"**: Quoted in Headington, 87–8.

57 **"He could make"**: Quoted in Blyth, 22.

57 **"Functioning as a"**: Quoted ibid., 132.

58 **Ann Beattie:** Dawn Trouard, ed., *Conversations with Ann Beattie* (Jackson: University Press of Mississippi, 2007).

58 **"I really think"**: Interview with Fred Sokol, *Connecticut Quarterly* 2, Summer 1980, in ibid., 24.

58 **"I really don't"**: Ibid., 25.

58 **"I certainly am"**: Margaria Fichtner, "Author Ann Beattie Lives in the Sunshine, but Writes in, and from, the Dark," *Miami Herald,* May 17, 1998, in Trouard, 171.

59 **Günter Grass:** Interview with Elizabeth Gaffney, "The Art of Fiction No. 124: Günter Grass," *Paris Review,* Summer 1991, http://www.theparisreview.org/interviews/2191/the-art-of -fiction-no-124-gunter-grass.

59 **Tom Stoppard:** Ira Nadel, *Tom Stoppard: A Life* (New York: Palgrave, 2002).

59 **"frightened enough to"**: Quoted ibid., 93.

59 **"An inveterate"**: Ibid., 436.

59 "intellectual inefficiency": Quoted ibid., 114.

60 "I never work": Quoted ibid., 484.

60 Haruki Murakami: Interview with John Wray, "The Art of Fiction No. 182: Haruki Murakami," *Paris Review*, Summer 2004, http://www.theparisreview.org/interviews /2/ the-art-of-fiction-no-182-haruki-murakami; Haruki Murakami, "The Running Novelist," *New Yorker*, June 9 & 16, 2008, 75.

60 "I keep to": Interview with Wray.

60 "Physical strength is": Ibid.

61 "People are offended": Murakami, 75.

61 Toni Morrison: Interview with Claudia Brodsky Lacour and Elissa Schappell, "The Art of Fiction No. 134: Toni Morrison," *Paris Review*, Fall 1993, http://www.theparis review.org/interviews/1888/the-art-of-fiction-no-134-toni -morrison; Danille Taylor-Guthrie, ed., *Conversations with Toni Morrison* (Jackson: University Press of Mississippi, 2004).

61 "I am not able": Interview with Lacour and Schappell.

61 "It does seem": Interview with Mel Watkins, "Talk with Toni Morrison," *New York Times Book Review*, September 11, 1977, in Taylor-Guthrie, 43.

62 "I am not very": Interview with Lacour and Schappell.

62 "watch the light": Ibid.

62 Joyce Carol Oates: Lee Milazzo, ed., *Conversations with Joyce Carol Oates* (Jackson: University Press of Mississippi, 1989).

63 "I write and": Interview with Leif Sjoberg, "An Interview with Joyce Carol Oates," *Contemporary Literature*, Summer 1982, in ibid., 105.

63 "Getting the first": Interview with Robert Compton, "Joyce Carol Oates Keeps Punching," *Dallas Morning News*, November 17, 1987, in Milazzo, 166.

63 Chuck Close: Interview with author, August 10, 2010.

64 Francine Prose: E-mail message to author's agent, Megan Thompson, April 20, 2009.

65 John Adams: Interview with author, May 20, 2010.

67 Steve Reich: Interview with author, January 25, 2010.

68 Nicholson Baker: Interview with author, August 6, 2010.

70 B. F. Skinner: B. F. Skinner, "My Day," August 9, 1963, B. F.

Skinner Basement Archives; Daniel W. Bjork, *B. F. Skinner: A Life* (New York: Basic Books, 1993).

70 "I rise sometime": Skinner, "My Day."

72 By the time: Bjork, 217.

72 Margaret Mead: Jane Howard, *Margaret Mead: A Life* (New York: Simon and Schuster, 1984).

72 "How dare they?": Quoted ibid., 287.

72 "Empty time stretches": Quoted ibid., 393.

73 Jonathan Edwards: George M. Marsden, *Jonathan Edwards: A Life* (New Haven: Yale University Press, 2003).

73 "I think Christ": Quoted ibid., 133.

73 "For each insight": Ibid., 136.

73 Samuel Johnson: James Boswell, *Life of Johnson* (1791; repr. Oxford: Oxford University Press, 1998); Peter Martin, *Samuel Johnson: A Biography* (Cambridge, MA: Harvard University Press, 2008).

73 "generally went abroad": Quoted in Boswell, 282.

74 "His general mode": Quoted ibid., 437.

74 "My reigning sin": Quoted in Martin, 458-9.

74 "idleness is a": Quoted in Boswell, 437.

75 James Boswell: James Boswell, *Boswell in Holland, 1763-1764*, ed. Frederick A. Pottle (1928; repr. New York: McGraw Hill, 1952); James Boswell, *Boswell's London Journal, 1762-1763*, ed. Frederick A. Pottle (New York: McGraw Hill, 1950).

75 "As soon as I": *Boswell in Holland*, 37.

75 "vile habit of": Ibid.

75 "I have thought of": Ibid., 198.

75 "My affairs are": *Boswell's London Journal*, 183-4.

76 "dreary as a": *Boswell in Holland*, 210.

76 "Everything is insipid": Ibid., 197.

77 "It gives me a": Ibid., 45.

77 "comforts and enlivens": *Boswell's London Journal*, 189.

77 "the dignity of": *Boswell in Holland*, 388.

77 "Life has much": Ibid., 389.

77 Immanuel Kant: Manfred Kuehn, *Kant: A Biography* (Cambridge, U.K.: Cambridge University Press, 2001).

77 "The history of Kant's life": Quoted ibid., 14.

78 "a certain uniformity": Quoted ibid., 153.

79 "Kant had formulated": Ibid., 222.

80 **William James:** Robert D. Richardson, *William James: In the Maelstrom of American Modernism* (Boston: Houghton Mifflin, 2006); William James, *Habit* (New York: Henry Holt, 1914).

80 **"Recollect," he wrote:** Quoted in Richardson, 121.

79 **the "great thing":** James, 54.

80 **"make our nervous":** Ibid.

81 **"James on habit":** Richardson, 240.

81 **"I know a":** Quoted ibid., 238.

82 **Henry James:** H. Montgomery Hyde, *Henry James at Home* (New York: Farrar, Straus and Giroux, 1969).

82 **"It's all *about*":** Quoted ibid., 152.

82 **Franz Kafka:** Franz Kafka, *Letters to Felice*, ed. Erich Heller and Jürgen Born, trans. James Stern and Elisabeth Duckworth (New York: Schocken Books, 1973); Louis Begley, *The Tremendous World I Have Inside My Head: Franz Kafka: A Biographical Essay* (New York: Atlas & Co., 2008).

82 **"single shift" system:** Begley, 29.

83 **"time is short":** Franz Kafka to Felice Bauer, November 1, 1912, in *Letters to Felice*, 21–2.

85 **James Joyce:** Richard Ellmann, *James Joyce* (1959; repr. Oxford: Oxford University Press, 1982); John McCourt, *James Joyce: A Passionate Exile* (London: Orion, 2000).

85 **"A man of":** Quoted in Ellmann, 6.

85 **"the mind is":** Quoted ibid., 308.

86 **"He woke about":** Ibid.

87 **"No," he replied:** Quoted in McCourt, 73.

87 **"diversified," as he put it:** Quoted ibid., 91.

87 **"I calculate that":** Quoted in Ellmann, 510.

87 **Marcel Proust:** Celeste Albaret and Georges Belmont, *Monsieur Proust*, trans. Barbara Bray (1973; repr. New York: New York Review Books, 2001); Ronald Hayman, *Proust: A Biography* (New York: HarperCollins, 1990); Marcel Proust, *In Search of Lost Time, Volume VI: Time Regained*, trans. Andreas Mayor, Terence Kilmartin, D. J. Enright (New York: Modern Library, 1993).

87 **"It is truly":** Quoted in Hayman, 346.

88 **"It isn't an":** Albaret and Belmont, 70.

89 **"After ten pages":** Quoted in Hayman, 251.

89 **"You're putting your":** Quoted ibid., 331.

90 "it almost seems": Proust, 318.

90 **Samuel Beckett:** Paul Strathern, *Beckett in 90 Minutes* (Chicago: Ivan R. Dee, 2005); Deirdre Bair, *Samuel Beckett: A Biography* (New York: Harcourt Brace Jovanovich, 1978).

90 "It was spent": Strathern, 45–6.

91 "dark he had": Ludovic Janvier quoted in Bair, 351.

91 "I shall always": Quoted in Bair, 352.

92 **Igor Stravinsky:** Stephen Walsh, *Stravinsky: A Creative Spring: Russia and France, 1882–1934* (New York: Alfred A. Knopf, 1999); Vera Stravinsky and Robert Craft, *Stravinsky in Pictures and Documents* (New York: Simon and Schuster, 1978).

92 "I get up at": Quoted in Walsh, 419.

92 "I have never": Quoted ibid., 115.

92 "rests the head": Quoted in Stravinsky and Craft, 298.

93 **Erik Satie:** Robert Orledge, *Satie Remembered* (Portland, OR: Amadeus Press, 1995).

93 "walked slowly": Quoted ibid., 69.

94 "the possibility of": Quoted ibid.

94 **Pablo Picasso:** John Richardson, *A Life of Picasso: The Cubist Rebel, 1907–1916* (New York: Alfred A. Knopf, 2007); Francoise Gilo and Carlton Lake, *Life with Picasso* (New York: McGraw Hill, 1964).

94 "After the shabby": Richardson, 43.

95 "He rarely spoke": Quoted ibid., 147.

95 "the artist veered": Ibid., 146.

96 "That's why painters": Quoted in Gilo and Lake, 116.

96 **Jean-Paul Sartre:** Annie Cohen-Solal, *Jean-Paul Sartre: A Life,* trans. Anna Cancogni, ed. Norman Macafee (1985; repr. New York: Dial Press, 2005); Deirdre Bair, *Simone de Beauvoir: A Biography* (New York: Touchstone, 1990).

96 "One can be": Quoted in Cohen-Solal, 286.

97 "His diet over": Ibid., 374.

97 "I thought that": Quoted ibid., 374–5.

97 **T. S. Eliot:** James E. Miller Jr., *T. S. Eliot: The Making of an American Poet, 1888–1922* (University Park: Pennsylvania State University Press, 2005); Allen Tate, ed., *T. S. Eliot: The Man and His Work* (New York: Delacorte Press, 1966); Lyndall Gordon, *T. S. Eliot: An Imperfect Life* (New York: W. W. Norton, 1999).

98 "I am sojourning": Quoted in Miller, 325.

98 "a figure stooping": Quoted in Tate, 3–4.

98 "I am now": Quoted in Miller, 278.

99 "the prospect of": Quoted in Gordon, 197.

99 **Dmitry Shostakovich:** Laurel E. Fay, *Shostakovich: A Life* (Oxford: Oxford University Press, 2000); Elizabeth Wilson, *Shostakovich: A Life Remembered* (Princeton, NJ: Princeton University Press, 1994).

99 "I always found": Quoted in Fay, 46.

100 "appeared to be": Quoted in Wilson, 194.

100 "I discovered him": Quoted ibid., 197.

100 "He would play": Quoted ibid.

101 "I worry about": Quoted ibid., 196.

101 **Henry Green:** Jeremy Treglown, *Romancing: The Life and Work of Henry Green* (New York: Random House, 2000); interview with Terry Southern, "The Art of Fiction No. 22: Henry Green," *Paris Review*, Summer 1958, http://www.theparisreview.org/interviews/4800/the-art-of-fiction-no-22-henry-green.

102 "Though he occasionally": Treglown, 95.

103 "Yes, yes, oh yes": Interview with Southern.

103 **Agatha Christie:** Agatha Christie, *An Autobiography* (New York: HarperCollins, 1977).

104 "The funny thing": Ibid., 431.

104 "All I needed": Ibid., 432.

104 "Many friends have": Ibid.

105 **Somerset Maugham:** Jeffrey Meyers, *Somerset Maugham: A Life* (New York: Alfred A. Knopf, 2004).

105 "Maugham thought that": Ibid., 37.

105 "When you're writing": Quoted ibid., 37–8.

105 **Graham Greene:** Norman Sherry, *The Life of Graham Greene, Volume Two: 1939–1955* (New York, Viking: 1994); Henry J. Donaghy, ed., *Conversations with Graham Greene* (Jackson: University Press of Mississippi, 1992).

106 "a nine-till-five": Christopher Burstall, "Graham Greene Takes the Orient Express," *The Listener*, November 21, 1969, in Donaghy, 60–1.

106 **Joseph Cornell:** Deborah Solomon, *Utopia Parkway: The Life and Work of Joseph Cornell* (New York: Farrar, Straus and Giroux, 1997).

109 **Sylvia Plath:** *The Unabridged Journals of Sylvia Plath, 1950–1962,* ed. Karen V. Kukil (New York: Anchor Books, 2000); Janet Malcolm, *The Silent Woman: Sylvia Plath and Ted Hughes* (1993; repr. New York: Vintage Books, 1995).

109 **"From now on":** Sylvia Plath, December 7, 1959, in *Journals,* 457.

109 **She was using:** Malcolm, 61.

109 **"I am a genius":** Quoted ibid., 61–2.

110 **John Cheever:** Blake Bailey, *Cheever: A Life* (New York: Alfred A. Knopf, 2009); John Cheever, *The Journals of John Cheever* (New York: Alfred A. Knopf, 1991).

110 **"When I was younger":** Quoted in Bailey, 92–3.

110 **"Almost every morning":** Ibid., 137.

111 **"achieve some equilibrium":** Cheever, 22–3.

111 **"The hours between":** Ibid., 277–8.

112 **"the horniest man":** Quoted in Bailey, 422.

112 **"two or three orgasms":** Quoted ibid., 433.

112 **"With a stiff prick":** Quoted ibid., 568.

112 **"I must convince":** Cheever, 255.

113 **Louis Armstrong:** Terry Teachout, *Pops: A Life of Louis Armstrong* (Boston: Houghton Mifflin Harcourt, 2009).

113 **described by Terry Teachout:** Ibid., 288–93.

114 **"It's been hard":** Quoted ibid., 371.

114 **W. B. Yeats:** Warwick Gould, John Kelly, and Deirdre Toomey, eds., *The Collected Letters of W. B. Yeats, Volume 2, 1896–1900* (Oxford: Clarendon Press, 1997); R. F. Foster, *W. B. Yeats: A Life, I: The Apprentice Mage, 1865–1914* (Oxford: Oxford University Press, 1997); Peter Kuch, *Yeats and A.E.: "The Antagonism That Unites Dear Friends"* (Totawa, NJ: Barnes and Noble Books, 1986).

114 **"I read from":** W. B. Yeats to Edwin Ellis, August 16, 1912, quoted in Foster, 468.

114 **According to another:** Kuch, 14.

114 **"Every change upsets":** W. B. Yeats to J. B. Yeats, November 1, 1898, in Gould et al., 282.

114 **"I am a very":** W. B. Yeats to William D. Fitts, August 19, 1899, in Gould et al., 439.

115 **"One has to give":** W. B. Yeats to Robert Bridges, June 6, 1897, in Gould et al., 111.

115 **Wallace Stevens:** Peter Brazeau, *Parts of a World: Wallace Stevens Remembered* (New York: Random House, 1983); Milton J. Bates, *Wallace Stevens: A Mythology of Self* (Berkeley and Los Angeles: University of California Press, 1985).

115 **"I find that":** Quoted in Bates, 157.

116 **Kingsley Amis:** Interview with Michael Barber, "The Art of Fiction No. 59: Kingsley Amis," *Paris Review*, Winter 1975, http://www.theparisreview.org/interviews/3772/the-art-of-fiction-no-59-kingsley-amis; Eric Jacobs, *Kingsley Amis: A Biography* (New York: St. Martin's Press, 1995).

116 **"Yes. I don't":** Interview with Barber.

117 **Amis's routine shifted:** Jacobs, 1–18.

118 **Martin Amis:** Interview with Francesca Riviere, "The Art of Fiction No. 151: Martin Amis," *Paris Review*, Spring 1998, http://www.theparisreview.org/interviews/1156/the-art-of-fiction-no-151-martin-amis.

118 **Umberto Eco:** Interview with Lila Azam Zanganeh, "The Art of Fiction No. 197: Umberto Eco," *Paris Review*, Summer 2008, http://www.theparisreview.org/interviews/5856/the-art-of-fiction-no-197-umberto-eco.

120 **Woody Allen:** Eric Lax, *Conversations with Woody Allen: His Films, the Movies, and Moviemaking* (New York: Alfred A. Knopf, 2007).

120 **"obsessive thinking":** Ibid., 119.

120 **"I've found over":** Ibid., 78.

121 **"I think in the":** Ibid., 117.

121 **David Lynch:** Richard A. Barney, ed., *David Lynch: Interviews* (Jackson: University Press of Mississippi, 2009); David Lynch, *Catching the Big Fish: Meditation, Consciousness, and Creativity* (2006; repr. New York: Jeremy P. Tarcher/Penguin, 2007).

121 **"I like things":** Quoted in Richard B. Woodward, "A Dark Lens on America," *New York Times Magazine*, January 14, 1990, in Barney, 50.

121 **"I have never":** Lynch, 5.

122 **"We waste so":** Ibid., 55.

122 **Maya Angelou:** Jeffrey M. Elliot, ed., *Conversations with Maya Angelou* (Jackson: University Press of Mississippi, 1989).

122 **"I try to keep"**: Interview with Walter Blum, "Listening to Maya Angelou," *California Living,* December 14, 1975, in Elliot, 153.

122 **"I usually get"**: Interview with Claudia Tate, *Black Women Writers at Work* (New York: Continuum, 1983), in Elliot, 40.

124 **"I have always"**: Quoted in Judith Rich, "Life Is for Living," *Westways,* September 1987, in Elliot., 79.

124 **George Balanchine**: Mason Francis, ed., *I Remember Balanchine: Recollections of the Ballet Master by Those Who Knew Him* (New York: Doubleday, 1991); Bernard Taper, *Balanchine: A Biography* (1984; repr. Berkeley and Los Angeles: University of California Press, 1996).

123 **"When I'm ironing"**: Quoted in Francis, 418.

124 **"My muse must"**: Quoted in Taper, 13.

125 **Al Hirschfeld**: Al Hirschfeld, *Hirschfeld On Line* (New York: Applause Books, 1999).

125 **"In his 90s"**: Mel Gussow, introduction to ibid., 18.

126 **"Very often, when"**: Louise Kerz Hirschfeld, "Looking Over His Shoulder," in Hirschfeld, 24.

126 **Truman Capote**: Interview with Pati Hill, "The Art of Fiction No. 17: Truman Capote," *Paris Review,* Spring–Summer 1957, http://www.theparisreview.org/interviews/4867/the-art-of-fiction-no-17-truman-capote.

127 **Richard Wright**: Hazel Rowley, *Richard Wright: The Life and Times* (New York: Henry Holt, 2001).

128 **As Hazel Rowley details**: Ibid., 153–5.

128 **"I never intend"**: Quoted ibid., 162.

129 **H. L. Mencken**: Fred Hobson, *Mencken: A Life* (New York: Random House, 1994); Carl Bode, ed., *The New Mencken Letters* (New York: Dial Press, 1977).

129 **"Like most men"**: H. L. Mencken to A. O. Bowden, April 12, 1932, in Bode, 262.

129 **"Looking back over"**: Quoted in Hobson, xvi–xvii.

130 **Philip Larkin**: Interview with Robert Phillips, "The Art of Poetry No. 30: Philip Larkin," *Paris Review,* Summer 1982, http://www.theparisreview.org/interviews/3153/the-art-of-poetry-no-30-philip-larkin; Philip Larkin, "Aubade," in *Collected Poems,* ed. Anthony Thwaite (1988; repr. New York: Farrar, Straus and Giroux, 1989).

130 **"I work all"**: Larkin., 208.

130 **"My life is"**: Interview with Phillips.

130 **"I was brought up"**: Ibid.

130 **"After that you're"**: Ibid.

131 **Frank Lloyd Wright:** Bruce Brooks Pfeiffer, ed., *Frank Lloyd Wright: The Crowning Decade, 1949–1959* (Fresno: California State University, 1989); David V. Mollenhoff and Mary Jane Hamilton, *Frank Lloyd Wright's Monona Terrace: The Enduring Power of a Civic Vision* (Madison: University of Wisconsin Press, 1999).

131 **"Between 4 and 7"**: Quoted in Mollenhoff and Hamilton, 113.

132 **"Perhaps it was"**: "Olgivanna Lloyd Wright on Her Husband," in Pfeiffer, 122.

132 **"I could not"**: Ibid.

132 **Louis I. Kahn:** Carter Wiseman, *Louis I. Kahn: Beyond Time and Style: A Life in Architecture* (New York: W. W. Norton, 2007).

132 **"Lou had so much"**: Quoted ibid., 87.

133 **George Gershwin:** Howard Pollack, *George Gershwin: His Life and Work* (Berkeley: University of California Press, 2006).

133 **"To me George"**: Quoted ibid., 175.

133 **"Like the pugilist"**: Quoted ibid.

133 **Joseph Heller:** Adam J. Sorkin, ed., *Conversations with Joseph Heller* (Jackson: University Press of Mississippi, 1993).

133 **"I spent two"**: Interview with Sam Merrill, *Playboy,* June 1975, in ibid., 163.

134 **"most intelligent"**: Quoted in Ann Waldron, "Writing Technique, Say Joseph Heller," *Houston Chronicle,* March 2, 1975, in Sorkin, 135.

134 **"I wrote for"**: Interview with Sam Merrill, *Playboy,* June 1975, in Sorkin, 165.

134 **"I am a chronic"**: Ibid., 161.

134 **"It's an everyday"**: Interview with Creath Thorne, *Chicago Literary Review: Book Supplement to the Chicago Maroon,* December 3, 1974, in Sorkin, 128.

134 **"I write very"**: Quoted in Curt Suplee, "Catching Up with Joseph Heller," *Washington Post,* October 8, 1984, in Sorkin, 239.

135 **James Dickey:** Henry Hart, *James Dickey: The World as a Lie* (New York: Picador USA, 2000).

135 **"Every time I":** Quoted ibid., 214–5.

135 **"If they said":** Quoted ibid., 215–6.

136 **"After five and":** Quoted ibid., 262.

136 **Nikola Tesla:** Margaret Cheney, *Tesla: Man Out of Time* (New York: Touchstone, 2001).

136 **"I've had many":** Quoted ibid., 54.

137 **Glenn Gould:** Kevin Bazzana, *Wondrous Strange: The Life and Art of Glenn Gould* (Oxford: Oxford University Press, 2004); Andrew Kazdin, *Glenn Gould at Work: Creative Lying* (New York: E. P. Dutton, 1989); Glenn Gould in *The Life and Times of Glenn Gould*, CBC Television, March 13, 1998, accessed on April 2, 2010, at http://www.youtube.com/watch?v=j1Mm_b5lHvU&feature=related.

137 **"most experienced hermit":** Quoted in Bazzana, 320.

138 **"I don't think":** Quoted ibid., 318.

139 **"I tend to follow":** Gould, CBC Television.

139 **"for Gould, everything":** Kazdkin, 25.

139 **"I don't approve of":** Quoted in Bazzana, 322.

140 **"best playing I do":** Quoted ibid., 326.

140 **"He was known":** Ibid., 321.

140 **"routinely ran to":** Ibid.

140 **fasting, he said:** Kazdin, 64.

141 **Louise Bourgeois:** Marie-Laure Bernadac and Hans-Ulrich Obrist, eds., *Louise Bourgeois: Destruction of the Father/ Reconstruction of the Father: Writings and Interviews 1923– 1997* (Cambridge, MA: MIT Press, 1998).

141 **"My life has":** Interview with Douglas Maxwell, *Modern Painters*, Summer 1993, in ibid., 239.

141 **"Each day is":** Louis Bourgeois, "Tender Compulsions," *World Art*, February 1995, in Bernadac and Obrist, 306.

141 **"I work like":** Louise Bourgeois, "Sixty-one Questions," 1971, in Bernadac and Obrist, 96.

141 **Chester Himes:** Michel Fabre and Robert E. Skinner, eds., *Conversations with Chester Himes* (Jackson: University Press of Mississippi, 1995).

141 **"I like to":** Michel Fabre, "Chester Himes Direct," *Hard-Boiled Dicks*, December 1983, in Fabre and Skinner, 130.

142 **Flannery O'Connor:** Brad Gooch, *Flannery: A Life of Flannery O'Connor* (New York: Little, Brown, 2009).

142 **"routine is a":** Quoted ibid., 222.

142 **"I may tear":** Quoted ibid., 225.

142 **"I go to bed":** Quoted ibid., 228.

143 **"I read a lot":** Quoted ibid.

143 **William Styron:** Interview with Peter Matthiessen and George Plimpton, "The Art of Fiction No. 5: William Styron," *Paris Review*, Spring 1954, http://www.theparisreview .org/interviews/5114/the-art-of-fiction-no-5-william-styron; James L. W. West III, ed., *Conversations with William Styron* (Jackson: University Press of Mississippi, 1985).

143 **"Let's face it":** Interview with Matthiessen and Plimpton.

143 **"I often have":** Interview with James L. W. West III, "A Bibliographer's Interview with William Styron," *Costerus*, 1975, in West, 204.

143 **"certain visionary moments":** Interview with Hilary Mills, "Creators on Creating: William Styron," *Saturday Review*, September 1980, in West, 241.

144 **"I think it's been":** Ibid., 240.

144 **Philip Roth:** David Remnick, "Into the Clear," *New Yorker*, May 8, 2000, 76–89; George J. Searles, ed., *Conversations with Philip Roth* (Jackson: University Press of Mississippi, 1992).

144 **"Writing isn't hard":** Quoted in Katharine Weber, "Life, Counterlife," *Connecticut*, February 1987, in Searles, 218.

145 **"I write from":** Quoted in Ronald Hayman, "Philip Roth: Should Sane Women Shy Away from Him at Parties?" *London Sunday Times Magazine,* March 22, 1981, in Searles, 118.

145 **"I live alone":** Quoted in Remnick, 79.

146 **P. G. Wodehouse:** Herbert Warren Wind, "Chap with a Good Story to Tell," *New Yorker*, May 15, 1971, 43–101; Robert McCrum, *Wodehouse: A Life* (New York: W. W. Norton, 2004).

146 **"I seem to":** Quoted in Wind, 45.

146 **"Wodehouse does his":** Wind, 89.

147 **"he might snooze":** McCrum, 405.

148 **Edith Sitwell:** Elizabeth Salter, *Edith Sitwell* (1979; repr.

London: Bloomsbury Books, 1988); Victoria Glendinning, *Edith Sitwell: A Unicorn Among Lions* (New York: Alfred A. Knopf, 1981).

149 **"the only time"**: Quoted in Salter, 16.

149 **"All women should"**: Quoted ibid., 17.

149 **"I am honestly"**: Quoted in Glendinning, 204.

149 **Thomas Hobbes**: John Aubrey, *Aubrey's Brief Lives,* ed. Oliver Lawson Dick (1949; repr. Ann Arbor: University of Michigan Press, 1957); Simon Critchley, *The Book of Dead Philosophers* (New York: Vintage Books, 2009).

149 **"threw himself immediately"**: Aubrey, 155.

150 **"he did believe"**: Ibid.

150 **John Milton**: John Aubrey, *Aubrey's Brief Lives,* ed. Oliver Lawson Dick (1949; repr. Ann Arbor: University of Michigan Press, 1957); Helen Darbishire, ed., *The Early Lives of Milton* (1932; repr. New York: Barnes and Noble, 1965).

150 **"would complain"**: John Phillips, "The Life of Mr. John Milton," in Darbishire, 33.

151 **René Descartes**: Jack Rochford Vrooman, *René Descartes: A Biography* (New York: G. P. Putnam's Sons, 1970).

151 **"Here I sleep"**: Quoted ibid., 76.

152 **Johann Wolfgang von Goethe**: David Luke and Robert Pick, eds., *Goethe: Conversations and Encounters* (London: Oswald Wolff, 1966).

152 **"At one time"**: Quoted ibid., 177.

152 **"My advice therefore"**: Quoted ibid., 178.

153 **Friedrich Schiller**: Heinrich Doering, *Friedrich von Schillers Leben*, in *Thomas Carlyle's Life of Friedrich Schiller*, facsimile ed. (Columbia, SC: Camden House, 1992); Bernt Von Heiseler, *Schiller*, trans. John Bednall (London: Eyre and Spottiswoode, 1962).

153 **"On his sitting"**: Doering, 111.

154 **"We have failed"**: Quoted in Von Heiseler, 103.

154 **Franz Schubert**: Otto Erich Deutsch, ed., *Schubert: Memoirs by His Friends*, trans. Rosamond Ley and John Nowell (London: Adam & Charles Black, 1958).

154 **"used to sit down"**: Anselm Hüttenbrenner, "Fragments from the Life of the Song Composer Franz Schubert," 1854, in ibid., 182.

154 **"Schubert never composed"**: Ibid., 183.

154 **"Schubert was extraordinarily"**: Leopold von Sonnleithner, November 1, 1857, in Deutsch, 109.

155 **Franz Liszt**: Adrian Williams, *Portrait of Liszt: By Himself and His Contemporaries* (Oxford: Clarendon Press, 1990).

155 **"He rose at four"**: Quoted ibid., 484.

156 **"To live one's"**: Quoted ibid., 482.

156 **George Sand**: George Sand, *Story of My Life: The Autobiography of George Sand: A Group Translation,* ed. Thelma Jurgrau (Albany: State University of New York Press, 1991).

156 **"If I did not"**: Ibid., 927.

157 **"It is said"**: Ibid., 928.

157 **Honoré de Balzac**: Herbert J. Hunt, *Honoré de Balzac: A Biography* (London: University of London, 1957); Graham Robb, *Balzac: A Life* (New York: W. W. Norton, 1994).

157 **"orgies of work"**: Hunt, 65.

158 **"The days melt"**: Quoted in Robb, 164.

158 **Victor Hugo**: Graham Robb, *Victor Hugo* (New York: W. W. Norton, 1997).

159 **"these were the days"**: Ibid., 404–5.

160 **"As soon as he"**: Quoted ibid., 406.

160 **Charles Dickens**: Peter Ackroyd, *Dickens* (New York: HarperCollins, 1990); Jane Smiley, *Charles Dickens* (New York: Viking Penguin, 2002).

160 **without certain conditions**: Ackroyd, 503, 561–2.

161 **Dickens's working hours**: Ibid., 561.

161 **"no city clerk"**: Quoted ibid.

161 **"searching for some"**: Quoted ibid., 563.

161 **"he looked the"**: Smiley, 23.

162 **Charles Darwin**: Francis Darwin, ed., *The Life and Letters of Charles Darwin,* vol. 1 (New York: Basic Books, 1959); "Charles Darwin," *Encyclopædia Britannica,* 2009, http://www.britannica.com/EBchecked/topic/151902/Charles -Darwin.

163 **the "extreme edge"**: *Encyclopaedia Britannica.*

163 **"like confessing"**: Ibid.

163 **a quiet, monkish life**: Darwin, 87–136.

164 **"I've done a"**: Quoted ibid., 91.

165 **"became extremely animated"**: Ibid., 101.

166 **"kind of restrained"**: Ibid., 121.

166 **Herman Melville**: Herman Melville, *Correspondence: The*

Writings of Herman Melville, vol. 14, ed. Lynn Horth (Evanston and Chicago: Northwestern University Press and the Newberry Library, 1993).

166 "I rise at eight": Herman Melville to Evert Duyckinck, December 13, 1850, in *Correspondence*, 174.

167 "I have a sort": Ibid., 173.

168 Nathaniel Hawthorne: Malcolm Cowley, ed., *The Portable Hawthorne*, rev. ed. (New York: Penguin Books, 1969); Randall Stewart, *Nathaniel Hawthorne: A Biography*, (1948; repr. North Haven, CT: Archon Books, 1970).

168 "As the years": Cowley, 2.

169 "I religiously seclude": Quoted in Stewart, 112.

169 Leo Tolstoy: Leo Tolstoy, *Tolstoy's Diaries*, ed. and trans. R. F. Christian (London: Flamingo, 1994); Sergei Tolstoy, *Tolstoy Remembered by His Son*, trans. Moura Budberg (New York: Atheneum, 1962); Tatyana Tolstoy, *Tolstoy Remembered*, trans. Derek Coltman (New York: McGraw-Hill, 1977).

169 "I must write": *Diaries*, 166.

170 "From September": Sergei Tolstoy, 53-4.

170 account by Tolstoy's daughter: Tatyana Tolstoy, 20.

171 "At five we": Sergei Tolstoy, 55.

171 Pyotr Ilich Tchaikovsky: David Brown, *Tchaikovsky: The Man and His Music* (New York: Pegasus Books, 2007); David Brown, *Tchaikovsky: The Final Years: 1855-1893*, (vol. 4) (New York: W. W. Norton, 1991).

171 "What a joy": Quoted in *The Man and His Music*, 284.

172 "was not only pleasure": Quoted in *The Final Years*, 19.

172 "Before setting about": Quoted ibid., 21.

172 "Somewhere at sometime": Quoted ibid.

172 "The seed of a": Quoted in *The Man and His Music*, 207.

173 "always found himself": Quoted in *The Final Years*, 22.

173 Mark Twain: Albert Bigelow Paine, *Mark Twain*, vol. 1 (1912; repr. New York: Chelsea House, 1997); William Dean Howells, *My Mark Twain*, rev. ed. (New York: Harper and Brothers, 1910; Mineola, NY: Dover Publications, 1997).

174 "On hot days": Quoted in Paine, 509.

174 "the whole house": Howells, 45.

174 "In those days": Ibid., 38-9.

175 **Alexander Graham Bell**: Charlotte Gray, *Reluctant Genius: Alexander Graham Bell and the Passion for Invention* (New York: Arcade Publishing, 2006).

175 **"It is hard work"**: Quoted ibid., 177.

176 **"I have my periods"**: Quoted ibid., 204.

176 **"I wonder do you"**: Quoted ibid., 265.

176 **Vincent van Gogh**: Vincent van Gogh, *The Complete Letters of Vincent van Gogh*, 3rd ed., vol. 3 (Boston: Bulfinch Press, 2000).

176 **"Today again from"**: Ibid., 48.

176 **"in a dumb fury"**: Ibid., 203.

176 **"Our days pass"**: Ibid., 101.

177 **N. C. Wyeth**: David Michaelis, *N. C. Wyeth: A Biography* (New York: Alfred A. Knopf, 1998).

177 **"fortified by grapefruit"**: Ibid., 293.

178 **"It's the hardest"**: Quoted ibid., 294.

178 **Georgia O'Keeffe**: John Loengard, *Georgia O'Keeffe at Ghost Ranch: A Photo Essay* (New York: Steward, Tabori and Chang, 1995); Lisa Mintz Messinger, *Georgia O'Keeffe* (London: Thames and Hudson, 2001); C. S. Merrill, *O'Keeffe: Days in a Life* (New Mexico: La Alameda Press, 1995).

178 **"I like to"**: Quoted in Loengard, 8.

178 **a typical meal**: Merrill, 23.

178 **"On the other"**: Quoted in Messinger, 182.

179 **"When I think"**: Quoted ibid.

179 **Sergey Rachmaninoff**: Sergei Bertensson and Jay Leyda, *Sergei Rachmaninoff: A Lifetime in Music* (New York: New York University Press, 1956).

179 **"Some pianists say"**: Quoted ibid., 295.

179 **"today I worked"**: Quoted ibid., 136.

180 **Vladimir Nabokov**: Vladimir Nabokov, *Strong Opinions* (1973; repr. New York: Vintage International, 1990); Vladimir Nabokov, "Nabokov on Nabokov and Things," *New York Times*, May 12, 1968, http://www.nytimes.com/books/97/03/02/lifetimes/nab-v-things.html.

180 **"I generally start"**: Interview with Alvin Toffler, *Playboy*, 1963, in *Strong Opinions*, 29.

181 **"I awake around"**: Ibid., 28-9.

181 **"My habits are simple"**: Interview with Allene Talmey, *Vogue,* 1969, in *Strong Opinions,* 157.

181 **"soccer matches"**: Interview with Kurt Hoffman in *Strong Opinions,* 191.

181 **"I sleep even worse"**: "Nabokov on Nabokov and Things."

182 **Balthus**: Balthus with Alain Vircondelet, *Vanished Splendors: A Memoir,* trans. Benjamin Ivry (New York: Ecco, 2002); Nicholas Fox Weber, *Balthus: A Biography* (New York: Alfred A. Knopf, 1999).

183 **"This is the"**: Balthus with Vircondelet, 3.

183 **"I've always painted"**: Ibid., 147.

184 **Le Corbusier**: Nicholas Fox Weber, *Le Corbusier: A Life* (New York: Alfred A. Knopf, 2008); Jerzy Soltan, "Working with Le Corbusier," http://www.archsociety.com/e107 _plugins/content/content.php?content.24.

185 **"The process of"**: Soltan.

185 **Buckminster Fuller**: J. Baldwin, *BuckyWorks: Buckminster Fuller's Ideas for Today* (New York: Wiley, 1996); Elizabeth Kolbert, "Dymaxion Man, " *New Yorker,* June 9, 2008, http:// www.newyorker.com/reporting/2008/06/09/080609fa_ fact_kolbert.

186 **"A series of trials"**: Baldwin, 66.

186 **"disconcerted observers"**: Ibid.

187 **Paul Erdős**: Paul Hoffman, *The Man Who Loved Only Numbers: The Story of Paul Erdős and the Search for Mathematical Truth* (New York: Hyperion, 1998).

187 **"he only needed"**: Quoted ibid., 256.

188 **"You've showed me"**: Quoted ibid., 16.

188 **"A mathematician"**: Quoted ibid., 7.

188 **Andy Warhol**: Pat Hackett, introduction to *The Andy Warhol Diaries* (New York: Warner Books, 1989).

189 **"Keeping to his"**: Hackett, xv–xvi.

192 **Edward Abbey**: David Petersen, ed., *Postcards from Ed: The Collected Correspondence of Edward Abbey, 1949–1989* (Minneapolis, Milkweed Editions, 2006).

192 **"When I'm writing"**: Edward Abbey to Morton Kamins, December 14, 1981, in ibid., 107–8.

192 **"I hate commitments"**: Edward Abbey to David Petersen, July 25, 1988, in Petersen, 152.

193 **V. S. Pritchett:** Jeremy Treglown, *V. S. Pritchett: A Working Life* (New York: Random House, 2004); *Complete Collected Essays* (New York: Random House, 1991).

193 **"Pritchett was a":** Treglown, 3.

193 **"clocked on":** Quoted ibid., 203.

194 **Edmund Wilson:** Lewis M. Dabney, *Edmund Wilson: A Life in Literature* (Baltimore: Johns Hopkins University Press, 2005); Jeffrey Meyers, *Edmund Wilson: A Biography* (Boston: Houghton Mifflin, 1995); Louis Menand, "Missionary," *New Yorker*, August 8, 2005, http://www.newyorker.com/archive/2005/08/08/050808crat_atlarge.

194 **"Wilson was the":** Dabney, 4.

194 **"at the Princeton club":** Quoted in Meyers, 48–9.

194 **"You have to set":** Quoted ibid., 77.

195 **"To write what":** Quoted in Menand.

195 **John Updike:** Interview with Zvonimir Radeljković and Omer Hadžiselimović, *Književna Smotra*, 1979, at http://www.newyorker.com/online/blogs/books/2009/10/american-centaur-an-interview-with-john-updike.html; interview with Charles Thomas Samuels, "The Art of Fiction No. 43: John Updike," *Paris Review*, Winter 1968, http://www.theparisreview.org/interviews/4219/the-art-of-fiction-no-43-john-updike; John Updike, introduction to *The Early Stories: 1953–1975* (2003; repr. New York: Ballantine Books, 2004); interview with the Academy of Achievement, June 12, 2004, http://www.achievement.org/autodoc/page/updoint-1.

195 **"I would write":** Interview with Samuels.

195 **"Around noon the":** Updike, xvii.

195 **"I try to":** Interview with Radeljković and Hadžiselimović.

196 **A solid routine:** Interview with the Academy of Achievement.

196 **Albert Einstein:** Ronald W. Clark, *Einstein: His Life and Times* (1971; repr. New York: Harper Perennial, 2007).

197 **"Einstein would pose":** Quoted ibid., 746.

197 **L. Frank Baum:** Katharine M. Rogers, *L. Frank Baum: Creator of Oz* (Cambridge, MA: Da Capo Press, 2002).

198 **"My characters just":** Quoted ibid., 179.

198 **Knut Hamsun:** Ingar Sletten Kolloen, *Knut Hamsun: Dreamer and Dissenter*, trans. Deborah Dawkin and Erik Skuggevik (New Haven, CT: Yale University Press, 2009).

198 **"A great deal"**: Quoted ibid., 127–8.

199 **Willa Cather**: L. Brent Bohlke, ed., *Willa Cather in Person* (Lincoln: University of Nebraska Press, 1986).

199 **"I work from two"**: Latrobe Carroll, "Miss Cather" in Bohlke, 23–4.

200 **Ayn Rand**: Anne C. Heller, *Ayn Rand and the World She Made* (New York: Nan A. Talese, 2009); Mary Ann Sures, "Working for Ayn Rand," in Mary Ann Sures and Charles Sures, *Facets of Ayn Rand*, Ayn Rand Institute, http://facets ofaynrand.com/book/chap1-working_for_ayn_rand.html.

200 **According to the**: Heller, 147.

200 **"She was very"**: Sures.

201 **George Orwell**: D. J. Taylor, *Orwell: The Life* (New York: Henry Holt and Company, 2003).

201 **Waking at 7:00**: Ibid., 148.

202 **Bachelor Griller**: Ibid., 155.

202 **James T. Farrell**: Robert K. Landers, *An Honest Writer: The Life and Times of James T. Farrell* (San Francisco: Encounter Books, 2004).

203 **"needed someone to"**: Quoted ibid., 405.

203 **Jackson Pollock**: Deborah Solomon, *Jackson Pollock: A Biography* (New York: Simon and Schuster, 1987); "Unframed Space," The Talk of the Town, *New Yorker*, August 5, 1950, 16.

204 **"I've got the"**: "Unframed Space."

205 **Carson McCullers**: Josyane Savigneau, *Carson McCullers: A Life*, trans. Joan E. Howard (1995; repr. New York: Houghton Mifflin, 2001); Virginia Spencer Carr, *The Lonely Hunter: A Biography of Carson McCullers* (Garden City, NY: Doubleday, 1975); Carson McCullers, *Illumination and Night Glare: The Unfinished Autobiography of Carson McCullers*, ed. Carlos L. Dews (Madison: University of Wisconsin Press, 1999).

205 **pact with her husband**: Savigneau, 56.

205 **McCullers wrote every day**: Carr, 78–9.

205 **McCullers later recalled**: McCullers, 18.

206 **Willem de Kooning**: Mark Stevens and Annalyn Swan, *De Kooning: An American Master* (New York: Alfred A. Knopf, 2005).

206 **"Typically, the couple"**: Ibid., 197–8.

208 **Jean Stafford**: Fern Marja Eckman, "Adding a Pulitzer to the Collection," *New York Post,* May 9, 1970, 21; David Roberts, *Jean Stafford: A Biography* (Boston: Little, Brown, 1988).

208 **"worn, patient"**: Eckman.

208 **"I'm a compulsive"**: Quoted ibid.

208 **"Does she write"**: Ibid.

209 **"I stay in"**: Quoted in Roberts, 384.

209 **Donald Barthelme**: Helen Moore Barthelme, *Donald Barthelme: The Genesis of a Cool Sound* (College Station: Texas A&M University Press, 2001).

210 **"the process of"**: Ibid., xiv.

210 **"during these first"**: Ibid., 94.

211 **Alice Munro**: Robert Thacker, *Alice Munro: Writing Her Lives: A Biography* (Toronto: Douglas Gibson, 2005).

211 **"very big on"**: Quoted ibid., 130.

211 **Jerzy Kosinski**: Interview with Rocco Landesman, "The Art of Fiction No. 46: Jerzy Kosinski," *Paris Review,* Summer 1972, http://www.theparisreview.org/interviews/4036/the-art-of-fiction-no-46-jerzy-kosinski; Jerzy Kosinski, *Blind Date* (New York: Grove Press, 1977).

211 **"When he was"**: Kosinski., 1.

212 **"I guess both"**: Interview with Landesman.

213 **Isaac Asimov**: Isaac Asimov, *I. Asimov: A Memoir* (New York: Doubleday, 1994).

213 **"The overriding factor"**: Ibid., 36.

213 **"I must have"**: Ibid., 38.

214 **Oliver Sacks**: E-mail message to author, March 17, 2010.

216 **Anne Rice**: Interview with author, January 27, 2011.

217 **Charles Schulz**: David Michaelis, *Schulz and Peanuts: A Biography* (New York: Harper, 2007).

218 **"just sit there"**: Quoted ibid., 370.

218 **"I would feel"**: Quoted ibid., 363.

218 **William Gass**: Theodore G. Ammon, ed., *Conversations with William H. Gass* (Jackson: University Press of Mississippi, 2003); Diane Ackerman, "O Muse! You Do Make Things Difficult!" *New York Times,* November 12, 1989, http://www.nytimes.com/books/97/03/02/reviews/ackerman-poets.html; interview with Thomas LeClair, "William Gass: The Art of Fiction No. 65," *Paris Review,* Summer 1977,

http://www.theparisreview.org/interviews/3576/the-art-of
-fiction-no-65-william-gass.

218 **In a 1998 interview:** Richard Abowitz, "Still Digging: A William Gass Interview," *Gadfly,* December 1998, in Ammon, 146.

218 **"'No, sorry to be":** Quoted in Ackerman.

218 **"I get very":** Interview with LeClair.

219 **David Foster Wallace:** David Lipsky, *Although of Course You End Up Becoming Yourself: A Road Trip with David Foster Wallace* (New York: Broadway Books, 2010); interview with Lewis Frumkes, 1999, http://lewisfrumkes.com/radioshow/david-foster-wallace-interview.

219 **"I usually go":** Quoted in Lipsky, 135. Commas added for consistency.

219 **"Things are either":** Interview with Frumkes.

219 **Marina Abramović:** Interview with author, August 12, 2010.

222 **Twyla Tharp:** Twyla Tharp with Mark Reiter, *The Creative Habit: Learn It and Use It for Life* (2003; repr. New York: Simon and Schuster Paperbacks, 2006).

222 **"I begin each":** Ibid., 14.

223 **"a friendly reminder":** Ibid., 15.

223 **"arsenal of routines":** Ibid.

223 **"I repeat the":** Ibid., 56.

223 **"It's actively anti-social":** Ibid., 237.

224 **Stephen King:** Stephen King, *On Writing* (2000; repr. New York: Pocket Books, 2002).

224 **"Like your bedroom":** Ibid., 152–3.

225 **Marilynne Robinson:** Interview with Sarah Fay, "The Art of Fiction No. 198: Marilynne Robinson," *Paris Review,* Fall 2008, http://www.theparisreview.org/interviews/5863/the-art-of-fiction-no-198-marilynne-robinson.

225 **Saul Bellow:** James Atlas, *Bellow: A Biography* (New York: Random House, 2000); Gloria L. Cronin and Ben Siegel, eds., *Conversations with Saul Bellow* (Jackson: University Press of Mississippi 1994); Saul Bellow, *Saul Bellow: Letters,* ed. Benjamin Taylor (New York: Viking, 2010). Kindle edition.

225 **"Someone once called":** Quoted in Nina Steers, "Successor to Faulkner," *Show,* September 1964, in Cronin and Siegel, 31.

226 "Rising promptly at": Atlas, 427.

226 "I simply get": Saul Bellow to Edward Shils, January 20, 1968, in *Letters*.

227 Gerhard Richter: Michael Kimmelman, "An Artist Beyond Isms," *New York Times*, January 27, 2002, http://www.nytimes.com/2002/01/27/magazinc/an-artist-beyond-isms.html.

227 Jonathan Franzen: Emily Eakin, "Into the Dazzling Light," *Observer*, November 11, 2001, http://www.guardian.co.uk/books/2001/nov/11/fiction.features; Nina Willdorf, "An Author's Story," *Boston Phoenix*, November 8–15, 2001, http://www.bostonphoenix.com/boston/news_features/other_stories/multi-page/documents/01997111.htm.

228 "I was frantically": Quoted in Willdorf.

228 "I was in such": Quoted in Eakin.

229 Maira Kalman: E-mail message to author, March 24, 2010.

229 Georges Simenon: Pierre Assouline, *Simenon: A Biography*, trans. Jon Rothschild (New York: Alfred A. Knopf, 1997); Patrick Marnham, *The Man Who Wasn't Maigret: A Portrait of Georges Simenon* (New York: Farrar, Straus and Giroux, 1992); interview with Carvel Collins, "The Art of Fiction No. 9: Georges Simenon," *Paris Review*, Summer 1955, http://www.theparisreview.org/interviews/5020/the-art-of-fiction-no-9-georges-simenon.

230 His typical schedule: Assouline, 326.

231 "Most people work": Quoted in Marnham, 163.

231 "Women have always": Interview with Collins.

233 Stephen Jay Gould: Interview with Academy of Achievement, June 28, 1991, http://www.achievement.org/autodoc/page/gouoint-1.

233 Bernard Malamud: Philip Davis, *Bernard Malamud: A Writer's Life* (Oxford: Oxford University Press, 2007); Lawrence Lasher, ed., *Conversations with Bernard Malamud* (Jackson: University Press of Mississippi, 1991); Janna Malamud Smith, *My Father Is a Book: A Memoir of Bernard Malamud* (New York: Houghton Mifflin, 2006); interview with Daniel Stern, "The Art of Fiction No. 52: Bernard Malamud," *Paris Review*, Spring 1975, http://www.theparisreview.org/interviews/3869/the-art-of-fiction-no-52-bernard-malamud.

233 "time-haunted man": Davis, 6.

233 **"absolutely, compulsively prompt"**: Malamud Smith, 36.

233 **"Discipline is an"**: Quoted in Jack Rosenthal, "Author Finds Room to Breathe in Corvallis," *Oregonian,* April 12, 1959, in Lasher, 9–10.

234 **"and I sneak"**: Quoted in Joseph Wershba, "Not Horror but Sadness," *New York Post,* September 14, 1958, in Lasher, 6.

234 **"There's no one"**: Interview with Daniel Stern.

INDEX

Page numbers in *italics* refer to illustrations.

PERMISSIONS ACKNOWLEDGMENTS

Grateful acknowledgment is made to the following for permission to reprint previously published material:

Alfred A. Knopf: Excerpt from *The Journals of John Cheever* by John Cheever. Copyright © 1990 by Mary Cheever, Susan Cheever, Benjamin Cheever, and Frederico Cheever. Reprinted by permission of Alfred A. Knopf, a division of Random House, Inc.

The B. F. Skinner Foundation: "My Day" by B. F. Skinner (August 9, 1963) from the B. F. Skinner Basement Archive. Reprinted by permission of The B. F. Skinner Foundation.

Doubleday: Excerpt from *I, Asimov: A Memoir* by Isaac Asimov. Copyright © 1994 by The Estate of Isaac Asimov. Reprinted by permission of Doubleday, a division of Random House, Inc.

Grand Central Publishing: Excerpt from *The Andy Warhol Diaries* by Andy Warhol and Pat Hackett. Copyright © 1989 by The Estate of Andy Warhol. Reprinted by permission of Grand Central Publishing as administered by the Hachette Book Group. All rights reserved.

McGraw-Hill Education: Excerpt from *Boswell's London*

Journal by James Boswell and Frederick Pottle. Reprinted by permission of McGraw-Hill Education.

Northwestern University Press: Excerpt from *Correspondence: The Writings of Herman Melville, Vol. 13* by Herman Melville, edited by Lynn Horth. Evanston: Northwestern University Press, 1993. Reprinted by permission of Northwestern University Press.

Schocken Books: Excerpt from *Letters to Felize* by Franz Kafka, edited by Erich Heller and Jurgen Born, translated by James Stern and Elizabeth Duckworth. Copyright © 1973 by Schocken Books, a division of Random House, Inc. Reprinted by permission of Schocken Books, a division of Random House, Inc.

PHOTO CREDITS/PERMISSIONS

148 Trinity Mirror/Mirrorpix/Alamy

162 The Complete Work of Charles Darwin Online (http://darwin-online.org.uk)/John van Wyhe, ed.

182 Martine Franck/Magnum Photos

189 Robert Levin/Corbis

207 Henry Bowden/Getty Images

230 Izis/*Paris Match*/Getty Images